# New England Cookbook

Delicious New England with Authentic
New England Recipes

By
BookSumo Press

Published by
http://www.booksumo.com

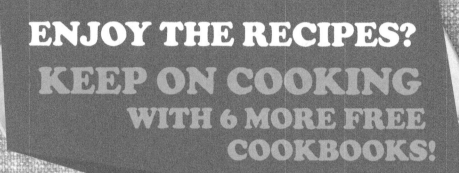

# LEGAL NOTES

# Table of Contents

# New England
# Clam Roast

Prep Time: 30 mins
Total Time: 1 hr 30 mins

Servings per Recipe: 8
| | |
|---|---|
| Calories | 485.9 |
| Fat | 20.7g |
| Cholesterol | 25.1mg |
| Sodium | 241.4mg |
| Carbohydrates | 64.3g |
| Protein | 11.9g |

## Ingredients

3 lb. crab claws
16 clams
8 new potatoes, quartered
8 corn on the cob, husked, each cut into thirds
2 medium onions, cut into pieces
1 C. parsley, chopped
1/4 C. basil leaf, torn
1 C. dry white wine

1/2 C. olive oil
1 tsp ground black pepper
1/2 tsp salt
2 tsp garlic, minced
1 tsp hot pepper sauce
3 bay leaves
1/4 C. butter

## Directions

1. Set your oven to 400 degrees F before doing anything else.
2. in a bowl, add the garlic, parsley, basil, white wine, olive oil, hot pepper sauce, salt and black pepper and mix until well combined.
3. In the bottom of a roasting pan, place the crab, followed by the clams, potatoes, corn, onions and garlic mixture evenly.
4. Top with the bay leaves. Cover the roasting pan and cook in the oven for about 30 minutes. Remove from the oven and stir the mixture well. Cover the roasting pan and cook for about 30 - 35 minutes, stirring once after 15 minutes.
5. Remove from the oven and discard the bay leaves.
6. Place the butter on top in the form of dots.
7. Enjoy hot.

# FISH AND CHIPS
## in New England

Prep Time: 10 mins
Total Time: 45 mins

Servings per Recipe: 4

| | |
|---|---|
| Calories | 782 kcal |
| Fat | 26.2 g |
| Carbohydrates | 91.9g |
| Protein | 44.6 g |
| Cholesterol | 125 mg |
| Sodium | 861 mg |

## Ingredients

1 C. all-purpose flour
1 tsp baking powder
Salt and black pepper, to taste
1 egg, beaten lightly
1 C. milk
4 large potatoes, peeled and cut into

strips lengthwise
4 C. vegetable oil
1 1/2 lbs cod fillets

## Directions

1. In a large bowl, add flour, baking powder, salt, black pepper, egg and milk.
2. Mix till well combined.
3. Keep everything aside for at least 20 minutes.
4. In a large bowl of chilled water, dip the potatoes for 2-3 minutes.
5. Drain the mix well and pat dry with paper towel.
6. In a large skillet, heat the oil with medium heat.
7. Add the potatoes and fry for about 3-4 minutes or till crisp and tender.
8. Transfer the potatoes onto a paper towel lined plate.
9. Coat the cod fillets in the flour mixture evenly.
10. Fry everything for about 3-4 minutes or till golden brown.
11. Transfer the cod fillets onto another paper towel lined plate.
12. Now, return the potato strips to the skillet and fry them for about 1-2 minutes more or till crispy.

# 3-Step
# Boston Baked Beans

Prep Time: 20 mins
Total Time: 4 hrs 20 mins

Servings per Recipe: 8
| | |
|---|---|
| Calories | 267.5 |
| Fat | 8.4g |
| Cholesterol | 11.5mg |
| Sodium | 834.4mg |
| Carbohydrates | 44.3g |
| Protein | 8.0g |

## Ingredients

4 slices turkey bacon, cooked crisply and crumbled
2 slices bacon, cooked soft
2 (16 oz.) cans baked beans, drained
1/2 green pepper, chopped
1/2 medium onion, chopped

1 1/2 tsp prepared mustard
1/2 C. ketchup
1/2 C. barbecue sauce
1/2 C. brown sugar, packed

## Directions

1. In the pot of a slow cooker, place all the ingredients except 2 soft bacon slices and gently, stir to combine.
2. Set the slow cooker on Low and cook, covered for about 8-12 hours.
3. Enjoy hot with a toping of the soft bacon slices.

# EASY
# Boston Crème Pie

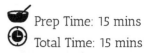

Prep Time: 15 mins
Total Time: 15 mins

Servings per Recipe: 8

| | |
|---|---|
| Calories | 340.2 |
| Fat | 13.9 g |
| Cholesterol | 41.0 mg |
| Sodium | 386.7 mg |
| Carbohydrates | 48.7 g |
| Protein | 5.6 g |

## Ingredients

16 oz. frozen pound cake, thawed and cut into three layers horizontally
1 (1 1/3 oz.) packages instant vanilla pudding

1 3/4 C. milk
1/2 C. chocolate fudge topping, chilled

## Directions

1. In a bowl, add the milk and pudding mix and beat until well combined.
2. Put the pudding mixture in the fridge for about 5 minutes.
3. Arrange the bottom layer of the cake onto a platter and top with 1/2 of the pudding mixture.
4. Now, arrange the middle layer of cake on top, followed by the remaining pudding and top layer of cake.
5. Now, spread the chocolate fudge topping over the cake evenly.
6. Put the cake in the fridge until set completely.
7. Enjoy chilled.

# *Potato*
# Chowder Bowls

Prep Time: 30 mins
Total Time: 1 hr

Servings per Recipe: 4
| | |
|---|---|
| Calories | 766.1 |
| Fat | 58.4g |
| Cholesterol | 202.5mg |
| Sodium | 1215.8mg |
| Carbohydrates | 32.6g |
| Protein | 28.8g |

## Ingredients

2 C. russet potatoes, peeled and cubed pieces
1 C. butter
2 tbsp diced green onions
1/4 C. flour
2 (6 1/2 oz.) cans minced clams
1 tsp salt
1 tsp black pepper

1 tsp garlic
12 oz. half-and-half
1/2 C. whole milk
1/3 C. clam juice
fresh parsley, minced

## Directions

1. In a pot of the water, add the potatoes over medium heat and cook until done through.
2. Drain the potatoes and keep aside.
3. In another pot, add the butter over medium-low heat and cook until melted.
4. Add the onion and cook for about 4-5 minutes.
5. Add the flour, beating continuously until smooth and thick.
6. Slowly, add half-and-half, beating continuously until creamy.
7. Add the potatoes, milk, bottled clam juice and clams with juice and cook until boiling.
8. Set the heat to low and cook for about 15 minutes, mixing frequently.
9. Enjoy hot.

# 10-MINUTE
# Lunch Box
# (Lobster Roll)

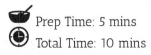 Prep Time: 5 mins

Total Time: 10 mins

Servings per Recipe: 1

| | |
|---|---|
| Calories | 171.5 |
| Fat | 12.0g |
| Cholesterol | 113.3mg |
| Sodium | 513.1mg |
| Carbohydrates | 0.4g |
| Protein | 15.0g |

## Ingredients

3 oz. lobster meat, per roll, cooked, cooled and chunked

1 - 2 tsp mayonnaise

salt and pepper

2 leaves lettuce, chopped

roll, split

1 tbsp margarine

## Directions

1. Set your grill and grease the grill grate.
2. In a bowl, add the lobster, mayonnaise, salt and mix well.
3. Spread the margarine onto rolls evenly.
4. Cook the roll onto the grill until crisp and golden brown.
5. Remove from the heat and arrange onto a platter.
6. Arrange the lettuce onto bottom half of each roll, followed by the lobster salad.
7. Cover with top half of the rolls and enjoy.

# Gloucester
# Chop Suey

Prep Time: 20 mins
Total Time: 50 mins

Servings per Recipe: 8
| | |
|---|---|
| Calories | 413.8 |
| Fat | 13.9g |
| Cholesterol | 50.0mg |
| Sodium | 473.2mg |
| Carbohydrates | 52.2g |
| Protein | 20.0g |

## Ingredients

3 tbsp butter
1 medium yellow onion, chopped
1 green bell pepper, stemmed, seeded, and chopped
2 garlic cloves, minced
1 lb. ground beef
1 tsp dried oregano
1 tsp dried basil
1/2 tsp ground black pepper

kosher salt
1 (14 1/2 oz.) cans diced tomatoes
1 (14 1/2 oz.) cans tomato sauce
1/4 C. tomato paste
2/3 C. tomato juice
1 pinch sugar
1 lb. elbow macaroni

## Directions

1. In a pan, add the butter over medium heat and cook until melted.
2. Add the bell pepper and onion and cook for about 4-6 minutes, mixing often. Add the garlic and cook for about 1 minute.
3. Add the ground beef and cook for about 9-10 minutes, breaking the meat with a spoon. Add the herbs, salt and pepper and stir to combine. Add the sugar, tomato paste, tomato juice, tomato sauce and canned tomatoes with their juices and cook for about 8-10 minutes.
4. Meanwhile, in a large pan of the salted boiling water, add the macaroni over high heat and cook until desired doneness, mixing often. Drain the macaroni well.
5. Add the macaroni into the meat mixture and gently, toss to coat well. Enjoy hot.

# 75-MINUTE
# Weeknight
# Chowder

 Prep Time: 15 mins
Total Time: 1 hr 15 mins

Servings per Recipe: 4
Calories               753.5
Fat                    40.2g
Cholesterol            144.5mg
Sodium                 1414.0mg
Carbohydrates          76.2g
Protein                24.3g

## Ingredients

6 - 7 pieces turkey bacon, cut into
pieces
1 medium onion, chopped
2 (5 oz.) cans baby clams, with juice
reserved
6 - 7 potatoes, cubed
2 (10 1/2 oz.) cans cream of celery
soup

1 C. heavy cream
1 C. milk
1 tbsp butter
1 tsp dried dill weed

## Directions

1.  Heat a pan over medium-low heat and cook the bacon until crispy.
2.  Add the onion and cook for about 4-5 minutes.
3.  Stir in the potatoes and the clam juice from cans and cook, covered for bout 18-20 minutes, mixing often.
4.  Add the clams, milk, cream, soup and dill weed and stir to combine.
5.  Add the butter and stir until melted.
6.  Cook for about 35-45 minutes, mixing often.
7.  Enjoy hot.

# Salma's
# Rice Pudding

Prep Time: 4 mins
Total Time: 16 mins

Servings per Recipe: 6
| | |
|---|---|
| Calories | 282.4 |
| Fat | 6.6g |
| Cholesterol | 78.4mg |
| Sodium | 177.8mg |
| Carbohydrates | 49.1g |
| Protein | 6.2g |

## Ingredients

3/4 C. sugar
2 tbsp cornstarch
1/4 tsp salt
2 C. milk
2 beaten eggs
2 C. cooked rice

1 tbsp butter
1 tsp vanilla
1/2 C. raisins
1 dash nutmeg

## Directions

1. In a pot, add the milk, cornstarch, sugar and salt over medium heat and cook for about 8-9 minutes, mixing continuously.
2. In a bowl, add the eggs and 2-3 tbsp of the hot milk mixture and beat vigorously until well combined.
3. Add the egg mixture into the pan, beating continuously.
4. Add the butter, raisins rice and vanilla and stir to combine.
5. Remove from the heat and keep aside for about 8-10 minutes.
6. Gently, stir the mixture and transfer into serving bowls.
7. Enjoy with a sprinkling of the nutmeg.

# FULL
# Clam Chowder

Prep Time: 20 mins
Total Time: 1 hr 5 mins

Servings per Recipe: 4

| | |
|---|---|
| Calories | 832.8 |
| Fat | 32.1g |
| Cholesterol | 127.3mg |
| Sodium | 2116.7mg |
| Carbohydrates | 98.0g |
| Protein | 38.1g |

## Ingredients

2 oz. bacon fat, optional
2 oz. butter
1 large onion, diced
6 stalks celery, diced
1 tbsp garlic, minced
1/2 shredded carrot
1/2 C. flour
1/2 C. instant mashed potatoes
4 chef potatoes, peeled and chopped
1 quart clam juice

3 C. chopped clams
1 1/2 C. half-and-half
1/4 C. parsley, chopped
1 drop Tabasco sauce
1/2 tsp celery salt
1/2 tsp thyme
1 bay leaf
2 tbsp chopped parsley

## Directions

1. In a pan, add the bacon fat and butter and cook until melted completely.
2. Add the carrots, celery, onion and garlic (and stir fry for about 4-5 minutes. Add the Tabasco sauce, parsley, thyme, bay leaf and celery salt and stir to combine.
3. Add the instant mash potatoes and flour and remove from the heat.
4. Now, stir until the flour is well combined.
5. Add the clam juice and mix well.
6. Place the pan over high heat and cook until boiling, mixing continuously.
7. Stir in the potatoes and cook for about 15 minutes.
8. Add the clams and cream and stir to combine.
9. Set the heat to low and cook for about 30 minutes, stirring occasionally.
10. Stir in the salt and pepper and remove from the heat.
11. Enjoy with a garnishing of the parsley.

# Sweet
# and Tangy Dijon Scallops

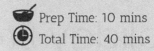 Prep Time: 10 mins

Total Time: 40 mins

Servings per Recipe: 4
Calories        257.3
Fat             15.3g
Cholesterol     67.6mg
Sodium          590.8mg
Carbohydrates   13.3g
Protein         16.3g

## Ingredients

2 - 3 slices turkey bacon
2 tbsp unsalted butter
1 lb. scallops
1 C. half - and - half

2 tbsp Dijon mustard
2 tbsp Vermont pure maple syrup

## Directions

1.  Heat a large skillet over medium - high heat and cook the bacon until browned completely.
2.  Transfer the bacon onto a paper towel lined plate to drain and then crumble it.
3.  Discard the bacon grease from the skillet.
4.  In the same skillet, add the butter over medium - high heat and cook until melted.
5.  Add the scallops and cook for about 3 minutes.
6.  With a slotted spoon, transfer the scallops into a warm bowl.
7.  Add the half - and - half into the skillet and cook until boiling, mixing often.
8.  Set the heat to medium and cook until mixture reduces to about 3/4 C.
9.  Stir in the maple syrup, mustard and any juices from the bowl of scallop bowl and cook for about 4 minutes, mixing frequently.
10. Add the crumbled bacon and scallops and toss to coat.
11. Enjoy hot.

# NOVEMBER
# Holiday Bread

Prep Time: 10 mins
Total Time: 1 hr 10 mins

Servings per Recipe: 16
Calories          314.8
Fat               9.4g
Cholesterol       0.0mg
Sodium            298.5mg
Carbohydrates     55.3g
Protein           3.2g

## Ingredients

3 1/2 C. all-purpose flour
1 2/3 C. sugar
2 tsp baking soda
1 tsp baking powder
3/4 tsp salt
1 tbsp cinnamon
1/2 tsp nutmeg
1/2 tsp allspice
1 tsp ginger
1 tsp vanilla extract

1 tsp orange extract
1 (16 oz.) cans whole berry cranberry sauce
1 (16 oz.) cans pumpkin
2/3 C. vegetable oil

## Directions

1. Set your oven to 350 degrees F before doing anything else and grease 2 (9-inch) loaf pans.
2. In a bowl, add the flour, sugar, baking soda, baking powder, spices and salt and mix well.
3. In another bowl, add the remaining ingredients and beat until well combined. Add the flour mixture and mix until just combined.
4. Cook in the oven for about 1 hour or until a toothpick inserted in the center comes out clean.
5. Remove from the oven and keep onto the wire racks to cool in the pans for about 10 minutes.
6. Carefully, invert the breads onto the wire racks to cool completely before slicing.
7. Meanwhile, for the glaze: in a bowl, add 1/4 C. orange juice concentrate, 1 C. of the powdered sugar and 1/8 tsp of the allspice and mix well.
8. Drizzle the glaze over both breads.
9. Cut into desired sized slices and enjoy.

# New England
# Hot Pea Soup

Prep Time: 15 mins
Total Time: 1 hr 15 mins

Servings per Recipe: 12

| | |
|---|---|
| Calories | 254.1 |
| Fat | 13.2g |
| Cholesterol | 0.0mg |
| Sodium | 1006.5mg |
| Carbohydrates | 31.8g |
| Protein | 6.1g |

## Ingredients

3 tbsp olive oil
1 tbsp chopped garlic
2 C. chopped onions
1 C. celery, minced
2 C. carrots, sliced
6 C. butternut squash, peeled and cut into chunks
2 C. canned tomatoes, diced
4 quarts well-flavored vegetable stock
2 C. tomato juice
1/2 C. soy sauce
1/4 C. fresh lime juice

2 C. canned chickpeas
1 tbsp ginger
1 tbsp ground coriander
1 tsp minced scotch bonnet pepper
1 (14 oz.) cans coconut milk
1 C. flaked coconut
1 tbsp cilantro, chopped
1 tsp coconut extract

## Directions

1. In a pan, add the olive oil and cook until heated.
2. Add the garlic and stir fry for about 1 minute.
3. Add the onions, celery and carrots and cook for about 12-15 minutes, mixing occasionally.
4. Add the chickpeas, squash, canned tomatoes, ginger, tomato juice, lime juice, soy sauce and coriander and cook until boiling.
5. Cook for about 28-30 minutes.
6. Stir in the cilantro, flaked coconut, coconut milk and coconut extract and cook until heated completely.
7. Enjoy hot.

# CHOPPED
# Cheese Cod

Prep Time: 15 mins
Total Time: 1 hr

Servings per Recipe: 4

| | |
|---|---|
| Calories | 414.9 |
| Fat | 25.5g |
| Cholesterol | 150.2mg |
| Sodium | 298.9mg |
| Carbohydrates | 7.3g |
| Protein | 37.8g |

## Ingredients

1 1/2 lb. cod
2 tbsp butter
1/2 C. chopped onion
2 tbsp flour

1 C. light cream
3/4 C. grated sharp cheddar cheese

## Directions

1. Set your oven to 350 degrees F before doing anything else and grease a Pyrex baking dish.
2. In a skillet, add the butter and cook until melted.
3. Add the onion and stir fry for about 2 minutes.
4. Add the flour, stirring continuously.
5. Add the cream, beating continuously and cook for about 1 minute.
6. Add the cheese and stir until melted.
7. In the bottom of the prepared baking dish,
8. arrange the fish fillets and top with the pour sauce.
9. Cook in the oven until till bubbly.
10. Enjoy hot.

# Creamy
# Rotini Roast

Prep Time: 20 mins
Total Time: 30 mins

Servings per Recipe: 4
| | |
|---|---|
| Calories | 360.8 |
| Fat | 8.1g |
| Cholesterol | 20.1mg |
| Sodium | 1362.1mg |
| Carbohydrates | 54.2g |
| Protein | 16.6g |

## Ingredients

1/2 lb. rotini pasta
1 (18 5/8 oz.) cans campbells select New England clam chowder
1/2 C. shredded cheddar cheese

1/2 tsp salt

## Directions

1. Set your oven to 350 degrees F before doing anything else.
2. In a pan of the salted boiling water, cook the Rotini pasta until desired doneness.
3. Meanwhile, in a pan, add the clam chowder and cook until heated completely, mixing often.
4. Drain the pasta completely and, transfer into a casserole dish.
5. Place the hot soup over the pasta, followed by the cheddar cheese.
6. Cook in the oven for about 10 minutes.
7. Enjoy hot.

# 15-MINUTE
# Pierogies

Prep Time: 5 mins
Total Time: 15 mins

Servings per Recipe: 6
| | |
|---|---|
| Calories | 82.1 |
| Fat | 3.5g |
| Cholesterol | 7.6mg |
| Sodium | 39.3mg |
| Carbohydrates | 12.6g |
| Protein | 2.3g |

## Ingredients

1 tsp Old Bay Seasoning
1/2 head green cabbage, quartered
2 ears corn, each cut in thirds
8 oz. low-fat beef kielbasa, sliced

1 1/2 tbsp butter, divided
1 (12 oz.) boxes frozen potato pierogis
parsley, chopped

## Directions

1.  In a Dutch Oven, add 1 C. of the water and Old Bay seasoning and cook until boiling.
2.  Add the kielbasa, corn, cabbage and 1/2 tbsp the butter and cook, covered for about 10 minutes, flipping twice.
3.  Meanwhile, in a microwave-safe bowl, add the pierogis and microwave for about 2 minutes.
4.  Add pierogis and remaining 1 tbsp butter and toss to coat well.
5.  Enjoy with a garnishing of the parsley.

# Weeknight
# Pot Roast

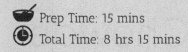 Prep Time: 15 mins

Total Time: 8 hrs 15 mins

Servings per Recipe: 6
Calories            789.3
Fat                 42.4g
Cholesterol         130.7mg
Sodium              638.1mg
Carbohydrates       58.0g
Protein             42.3g

## Ingredients

2 1/2 lb. beef chuck roast, fat removed
3 C. baby carrots
1 yellow onion, quartered
1 C. celery, diced
5 large red potatoes, halved
1/3 C. minced onion
2 tbsp apple cider vinegar
1 bay leaf

2 tbsp olive oil
1 1/2 tbsp horseradish
3 C. beef broth
1/2 tsp kosher salt
1/2 tsp black pepper

## Directions

1. In a greased crock pot, add all the ingredients and stir to combine.
2. Set the crock pot on low and cook for about 6-8 hours.
3. Enjoy hot.

# CLAM
# Chowder 101

🥣 Prep Time: 10 mins
🕐 Total Time: 50 mins

Servings per Recipe: 4

| | |
|---|---|
| Calories | 364.8 |
| Fat | 14.5g |
| Cholesterol | 32.5mg |
| Sodium | 368.3mg |
| Carbohydrates | 47.8g |
| Protein | 13.6g |

## Ingredients

6 slices thick turkey bacon, cut
crosswise into pieces
1 large onion, chopped
2 large carrots, peeled & chopped
1 1/4 tsp dried thyme
3/4 tsp crushed dried rosemary
3 tbsp all-purpose flour

4 C. whole milk
1 (8 oz.) unpeeled white potatoes, cubed
3 (6 1/2 oz.) cans chopped clams with
juice
1 (8 3/4 oz.) cans corn, drained
chopped parsley

## Directions

1. Heat a large skillet on medium heat and cook the bacon till browned completely.
2. Transfer the bacon onto a paper towel lined plate to drain and then crumble it. Remove the bacon grease from the skillet, leaving 3 tbsp inside. Add the onion, carrots, thyme, rosemary, salt and pepper and stir dry for about 6 minutes.
3. Stir in the flour and cook for about 1-2 minutes, mixing continuously.
4. slowly, add the milk, mixing continuously.
5. Cook until boiling.
6. Set the heat to medium and cook for about 5 minutes, mixing often.
7. Add the corn, potatoes and clams with juice and cook until boiling.
8. Set the heat to medium-low and cook for about 10 minutes, mixing occasionally.
9. Stir in the salt and pepper and enjoy hot with a topping of the bacon and parsley.

# Amherst
# Seafood Burgers

Prep Time: 30 mins
Total Time: 45 mins

Servings per Recipe: 2
| | |
|---|---|
| Calories | 768.1 |
| Fat | 40.0g |
| Cholesterol | 324.9mg |
| Sodium | 1953.2mg |
| Carbohydrates | 55.7g |
| Protein | 46.7g |

## Ingredients

Cakes
1 slice bread, dried crusts removed and torn
1/8 C. milk
1/2 tbsp mayonnaise
1/2 tbsp Worcestershire sauce
1/2 tbsp parsley flakes
1/2 tbsp baking powder
1/2 tsp Old Bay Seasoning
1/8 tsp salt
1/2 tbsp lemon juice
1 egg, beaten
1/2 lb. crab-meat, pricked
1 tbsp butter
1 tbsp oil
Filling

2 oz. cheddar cheese, sliced
6 tbsp onions, caramelized
3 1/2 oz. shrimp, boiled
2 slices tomatoes, sliced
4 pieces frisee
Tartar Sauce
1/4 C. mayonnaise
1/8 C. sweet pickle relish, drained
2/3 tsp instant minced onion
2/3 tsp lemon juice
1/4 tbsp sugar
1/2 tsp celery seed
1/2 tsp garlic powder
Bread
4 slices white bread, thick slices toasted

## Directions

1. In a bowl, add the bread pieces and milk and toss to coat well. In another bowl, add the eggs and beat well. Add the mayonnaise, lemon juice, Worcestershire sauce, baking powder and seasonings and mix well. Add the crab meat and mix until just combined.

2. Make a burger from the mixture. Place in the fridge for about 35-40 minutes.

3. In a skillet, add the oil and butter and cook until just heated. Place the crab burger and until brown from both sides. Meanwhile, for the sauce: in a bowl, add all the ingredients and mix well.

4. Place the burger onto a bread slice roll with your favorite condiments. Cover with other bread slice and enjoy alongside the tartar sauce.

# CHOCOLATE CHIP
# Muffins

Prep Time: 10 mins
Total Time: 30 mins

Servings per Recipe: 12
| | |
|---|---|
| Calories | 232.7 |
| Fat | 8.7g |
| Cholesterol | 28.1mg |
| Sodium | 311.4mg |
| Carbohydrates | 37.0g |
| Protein | 4.2g |

## Ingredients

1 C. all-purpose flour
1 C. whole wheat pastry flour
2/3 C. brown sugar
1/2 tsp salt
2 tsp baking powder
1 tsp baking soda
1 C. chocolate chips

1 large egg
3/4 C. skim milk
1 C. nonfat vanilla yogurt
1/4 C. butter, melted
1 tsp vanilla

## Directions

1. Set your oven to 375 degrees F before doing anything else and lightly, grease 12 cups of a muffin pan.
2. In a bowl, add the flours, brown sugar, baking powder, baking soda and salt and mix well.
3. Add chocolate chips and stir to combine well.
4. In a second bowl, add the butter, yogurt, milk, egg and vanilla and beat until well combined.
5. With your hands, make a well in the center of the flour mixture.
6. Add the egg mixture into the well and mix until just combined.
7. Place the mixture into the prepared muffin cups evenly.
8. Cook in the oven for about 18-20 minutes.
9. Remove from the oven and keep onto the wire rack to cool in the pans for about 5 minutes.
10. Carefully, invert the muffins onto the wire racks to cool completely.
11. Enjoy.

# Rhode Island
# Gratin

Prep Time: 30 mins
Total Time: 1 hr 25 mins

Servings per Recipe: 6
| | |
|---|---|
| Calories | 180.6 |
| Fat | 2.4g |
| Cholesterol | 5.9mg |
| Sodium | 321.1mg |
| Carbohydrates | 30.5g |
| Protein | 10.9g |

## Ingredients

6 C. cabbage, chopped
3 medium potatoes, unpeeled, cubed
2 C. carrots, sliced
1 1/2 C. leeks, white part only, sliced
1 tsp caraway seed
2 tsp paprika
1/2 tsp garlic powder
1/4 tsp salt

1/4 tsp pepper
2 C. water
6 oz. shredded low-fat cheddar cheese

## Directions

1. In a Dutch oven, add the potatoes, carrots, cabbage, leeks, spices and water over medium heat and cook until boiling, mixing often.
2. Set the heat to low and cook, covered for about 28-30 minutes.
3. Meanwhile, set your oven to 350 degrees F.
4. remove the pan from the heat and top the vegetable mixture with the cheese evenly.
5. Cover the pan and cook in the oven for about 25 minutes.
6. Enjoy hot.

# SPORTS BAR
# Seafood Dip

Prep Time: 2 hrs 9 mins
Total Time: 2 hrs 9 mins

Servings per Recipe: 6

| | |
|---|---|
| Calories | 105.5 |
| Fat | 6.8g |
| Cholesterol | 53.2mg |
| Sodium | 299.5mg |
| Carbohydrates | 4.6g |
| Protein | 6.4g |

## Ingredients

1/2 lb. lobster meat, cooked, chopped
1/2 C. mayonnaise
chives
pepper

cracker

## Directions

1. In a bowl, add all the ingredients except the crackers and mix until well combined.
2. Cover the bowl and place in the fridge for about 3 hours.
3. Enjoy over the crackers.

# Cinnamon
# Clove Cakes

🥄 Prep Time: 15mins
🕐 Total Time: 40 mins

Servings per Recipe: 12
| | |
|---|---|
| Calories | 277.4 |
| Fat | 9.3g |
| Cholesterol | 53.4mg |
| Sodium | 215.2mg |
| Carbohydrates | 44.7g |
| Protein | 4.3g |

## Ingredients

2 1/2 C. flour
2 1/2 tsp baking powder
1/4 tsp salt
1 tsp cinnamon
1/2 tsp mace
1/4 tsp clove
1/2 C. butter

1 C. sugar
2 eggs
1/3 C. molasses
3/4 C. milk

## Directions

1. Set your oven to 350 degrees F before doing anything else and grease 2 (9-inch) round cake pans.
2. In a bowl, add the flour, baking powder, cinnamon, clove, mace and salt and mix well.
3. Now, sift the flour mixture into a second bowl.
4. In another bowl, add the sugar and butter and beat until creamy.
5. Add the eggs, one at a time and beat until well combined.
6. Add the molasses and mix well.
7. Add the flour mixture, alternately with the milk and beat until well combined.
8. Place the mixture into the prepared cake pans evenly.
9. Cook in the oven for about 25 minutes or until a toothpick inserted in the center comes out clean.
10. Remove from the oven and keep onto the wire racks to cool in the pans for about 1 minute.
11. Carefully, invert the breads onto the wire rack to cool completely.
12. Cut into desired sized slices and enjoy.

# HOW TO MAKE
# Cocktail Sauce

Prep Time: 10 mins
Total Time: 10 mins

Servings per Recipe: 4
| | |
|---|---|
| Calories | 49.6 |
| Fat | 0.2g |
| Cholesterol | 0.0mg |
| Sodium | 531.6mg |
| Carbohydrates | 14.2g |
| Protein | 1.1g |

## Ingredients

2/3 C. ketchup
1/2 tbsp Worcestershire sauce
2 - 3 tbsp horseradish
1/4 tsp Tabasco sauce
1 tsp clam broth
1/4 tsp ground pepper
1/2 tsp dry mustard

1 pinch salt
1 lemon

## Directions

1. In a bowl, add all the ingredients except the lemon juice and stir to combine.
2. Add juice of 1/2 of the lemon and mix well.
3. Place in the fridge for about 1 1/2 - 2 hours.
4. Enjoy with a drizzling of the juice of remaining lemon.

# Orzo Cauldron

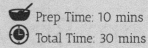 Prep Time: 10 mins

Total Time: 30 mins

Servings per Recipe: 12

| | |
|---|---|
| Calories | 149.5 |
| Fat | 4.8g |
| Cholesterol | 124.0mg |
| Sodium | 799.9mg |
| Carbohydrates | 14.0g |
| Protein | 11.7g |

## Ingredients

3 quarts chicken broth
1 C. dried orzo pasta
1/2 lb. asparagus, sliced
8 eggs, beaten
2 lemons, juice

1 bunch scallion, chopped
4 -6 dashes lemon extract
ground black pepper

## Directions

1. In a pan, add the chicken stock and cook until boiling.
2. Stir in the orzo and cook for about 6-7 minutes.
3. Add the asparagus and cook for about 6-7 minutes.
4. Slowly, add the beaten eggs, beating continuously.
5. Cook for about 1 minute.
6. Remove from the heat and stir in the remaining ingredients.
7. Enjoy hot.

# NEW ENGLAND
# Clam Bowls

Prep Time: 10 mins
Total Time: 50 mins

Servings per Recipe: 3
| | |
|---|---|
| Calories | 436.0 |
| Fat | 26.5g |
| Cholesterol | 110.1mg |
| Sodium | 1986.9mg |
| Carbohydrates | 30.1g |
| Protein | 20.2g |

## Ingredients

2 tbsp butter
1 C. diced onion
1/2 C. diced celery
1/2 C. diced leek
1/4 tsp chopped garlic
2 tbsp flour
1 quart milk

1 C. minced clams with juice
1 C. diced potato
1 tbsp salt
1/4 tsp white pepper
1 tsp dried thyme
1/2 C. heavy cream

## Directions

1. In a pan, add the butter over medium heat until heated.
2. Add the celery, leeks, onion and garlic and stir fry for about 3 minutes, stirring occasionally.
3. Remove from the heat and immediately, add the flour, stirring continuously until well combined.
4. Add the milk, beating continuously until smooth.
5. Drain the clams and add the juice into the soup.
6. Cook until boiling, mixing continuously.
7. Add the potatoes and seasonings and stir to combine.
8. Set the heat to low and cook for about 9-10 minutes.
9. Stir in the clams and cook for about 6-8 minutes.
10. Stir in the heavy cream and enjoy.

# Sweet Maple
# Muffins

🥣 Prep Time: 15 mins
🕐 Total Time: 35 mins

Servings per Recipe: 12
| | |
|---|---|
| Calories | 177.9 |
| Fat | 4.6g |
| Cholesterol | 28.5mg |
| Sodium | 156.7mg |
| Carbohydrates | 31.5g |
| Protein | 2.8g |

## Ingredients

1 3/4 C. all-purpose flour
1 tsp baking soda
1/2 tsp baking powder
1/2 C. granulated sugar
1/4 C. melted butter
1 egg, beaten
1 tsp vanilla extract

2 medium bananas, mashed
4 tbsp milk
4 tbsp maple syrup

## Directions

1. Set your oven to 375 degrees F before doing anything else and grease 12 cups of a muffin pan.
2. In a bowl, add the flour, baking powder and baking soda and mix well.
3. Now, sift the flour mixture into another bowl.
4. Add the sugar and mix well.
5. In a third bowl, add the milk, melted butter, egg, maple syrup, vanilla extract and bananas and beat until combined nicely.
6. Add the flour mixture and mix until just combined.
7. Place the mixture into the prepared muffin cups evenly.
8. Cook in the oven for about 20 minutes.
9. Enjoy warm.

# TRADITIONAL
# English Egg Scramble (Kedgeree)

 Prep Time: 20 mins

Total Time: 25 mins

Servings per Recipe: 6

| | |
|---|---|
| Calories | 190.9 |
| Fat | 9.8g |
| Cholesterol | 163.4mg |
| Sodium | 436.4mg |
| Carbohydrates | 18.8g |
| Protein | 6.1g |

## Ingredients

2 C. cooked rice
2 C. flaked cooked fish
4 hard-boiled eggs, chopped
2 tbsp minced parsley
1/2 C. cream

1 tsp salt
1/8 tsp pepper

## Directions

1.  In a pan, add all the ingredients and cook until heated through.

2.  Enjoy hot.

# Simple
# Onion Soup

 Prep Time: 10 mins

Total Time: 20 mins

Servings per Recipe: 4

| | |
|---|---|
| Calories | 249.0 |
| Fat | 13.2g |
| Cholesterol | 115.3mg |
| Sodium | 1075.1mg |
| Carbohydrates | 23.7g |
| Protein | 9.8g |

## Ingredients

2 tbsp butter
4 large onions, sliced
2 tbsp flour
2 C. milk
2 C. chicken broth
1 tsp salt
1/2 tsp pepper

1/2 tsp mace
2 egg yolks
parsley, minced

## Directions

1. In a pan, add the butter and cook until melted.
2. Add the onions and stir fry for about 5-6 minutes.
3. Add the flour and mix until well combined.
4. Slowly, add the milk, mixing continuously until smooth.
5. Stir in the broth and seasonings and cook for about 4-5 minutes.
6. Meanwhile, in a bowl, add the cream and egg yolks and beat until well combined.
7. Slowly, add the cream mixture into soup, stirring continuously.
8. Enjoy hot with a garnishing of the parsley.

# MUFFIN
# Mondays

Prep Time: 20 mins
Total Time: 50 mins

Servings per Recipe: 1
| | |
|---|---|
| Calories | 171.0 |
| Fat | 6.6g |
| Cholesterol | 46.1mg |
| Sodium | 233.3mg |
| Carbohydrates | 24.9g |
| Protein | 2.9g |

## Ingredients

1 1/2 C. flour
3/4 C. sugar
1 tsp baking powder
1/2 tsp baking soda
1/2 tsp cinnamon
1/2 tsp salt
2 eggs

4 tbsp butter, melted
1/2 C. sour cream
1 tsp vanilla
1/3 C. full cranberry-orange relish

## Directions

1. Set your oven to 350 degrees F before doing anything else and line cups of muffin pans with the paper liners.
2. In a bowl, add the flour, sugar, baking soda, baking powder, cinnamon and salt and mix well.
3. In a second bowl, add the sour cream, butter, eggs and vanilla and beat until well combined.
4. Make a well in the center of the flour mixture.
5. In the well, add the egg mixture and mix until just combined.
6. Add the cranberry relish and gently, stir to combine.
7. Place the mixture into the prepared muffin cups evenly.
8. Cook in the oven for about 20-30 minutes.
9. Remove from the oven and keep onto the wire rack to cool in the pans for about 5 minutes.
10. Carefully, invert the muffins onto the wire racks to cool completely.
11. Enjoy.

# Burlington
# Weeknight Burgers

Prep Time: 15 mins
Total Time: 35 mins

Servings per Recipe: 4
| | |
|---|---|
| Calories | 395.4 |
| Fat | 9.0g |
| Cholesterol | 148.4mg |
| Sodium | 175.1mg |
| Carbohydrates | 40.1g |
| Protein | 38.1g |

## Ingredients

1 tbsp unsalted butter
1 McIntosh apple, cored, quartered and chopped
1 small onion, chopped
2 celery ribs, chopped
1 tsp poultry seasoning
salt & ground black pepper
1 1/4 lb. ground turkey breast
1 egg

1/4 C. breadcrumbs
flat leaf parsley, chopped
1 tbsp olive oil
1 C. whole berry cranberry sauce
1 tbsp grated orange zest
2 scallions, chopped

## Directions

1. In a nonstick skillet, add 1 tbsp of the butter over medium heat and cook until melted. Add the apple, celery, onion, poultry seasoning, salt and pepper and cook for about 5-6 minutes, mixing often.
2. Remove from the heat and place the onion mixture into a bowl.
3. Keep aside to cool for about 5 minutes.
4. Add the turkey, parsley, breadcrumbs, egg, salt and pepper and with a fork, mix well.
5. Make 4 (4-inch) patties from the mixture.
6. In another skillet, add the olive oil over medium heat and cook until heated through.
7. Add the patties and cook for about 12 minutes, flipping once half way through, reducing the heat to low in the last 2-3 minutes of cooking.
8. Meanwhile, for the relish: in a bowl, add the cranberry sauce, scallions and orange zest and mix until well combined.
9. Enjoy the burgers alongside the cranberry relish.

# POT PIE
# Americana

Prep Time: 50 mins
Total Time: 1 hr 30 mins

Servings per Recipe: 6
| | |
|---|---|
| Calories | 524.3 |
| Fat | 25.7g |
| Cholesterol | 78.8mg |
| Sodium | 998.4mg |
| Carbohydrates | 43.4g |
| Protein | 29.3g |

## Ingredients

1 1/4 lb. boneless chicken breasts
4 C. chicken broth
12 white pearl onions
1 1/2 C. potatoes, diced
1 C. celery, diced
1 C. frozen peas
1 C. diced carrot
1 tbsp butter

5 tbsp flour
1/2 C. light cream
1 dash cracked pepper
1/2 tsp tarragon
1/2 tsp salt
1 premade pie crust

## Directions

1. In a pan of the water, add the chicken and cook for about 22-25 minutes. Drain well and keep aside to cool.
2. Then, cut the chicken into chunks and keep aside.
3. Set your oven to 400 degrees F. In a pan, add the broth and cook until boiling. Stir in the onions, celery, tarragon, salt and pepper and cook for about 4-5 minutes. Stir in the carrots and potatoes and cook for about 9-10 minutes. Drain the vegetables, reserving the broth. In another pan, add the broth and cook until boiling.
4. Add the flour and butter, beating continuously until mixture just begins to thicken.
5. Stir in the cream and cook until boiling.
6. In a casserole dish, place the chicken chunks, followed by the peas, cooked veggie mixture and broth mixture.
7. Place the premade pie crust on top and with a fork, poke holes at many places.
8. Cook in the oven for about 30-40 mins
9. Enjoy warm.

# Hartford
# Spud Cakes

 Prep Time: 10 mins

Total Time: 20 mins

Servings per Recipe: 3
| | |
|---|---|
| Calories | 275.7 |
| Fat | 10.7g |
| Cholesterol | 116.2mg |
| Sodium | 329.4mg |
| Carbohydrates | 23.3g |
| Protein | 20.6g |

## Ingredients

1 (7 oz.) cans sockeye salmon
1 C. mashed potatoes
1 C. frozen peas
1 egg, beaten
1 green onion, chopped, green & white parts
2 tbsp Mrs. dash chicken, grilling

seasoning blend
2 tbsp flour
1 tsp butter
1 tsp vegetable oil

## Directions

1. In a bowl, add all the ingredients except the flour, butter and oil and mix until well combined.
2. Make 6 patties from the salmon mixture and then, coat each with flour evenly.
3. In a skillet, add the oil and butter over medium heat and cook until heated through.
4. Add patties and cook for about 10 minutes, flipping once half way through.
5. Enjoy hot.

# 7-INGREDIENT
# Chowder

Prep Time: 10 mins
Total Time: 30 mins

Servings per Recipe: 8

| | |
|---|---|
| Calories | 246.5 |
| Fat | 5.3g |
| Cholesterol | 86.0mg |
| Sodium | 747.4mg |
| Carbohydrates | 16.1g |
| Protein | 31.6g |

## Ingredients

1/2 C. diced turkey bacon
1/2 C. minced onion
2 (10 1/2 oz.) cans cream of potato soup
1 1/2 C. milk

2 tbsp lemon juice
4 (8 oz.) cans minced clams
1/4 tsp pepper

## Directions

1. Heat a pot and cook the onion and bacon for about 8-10 minutes.
2. Stir in the milk and soup and cook until heated completely, mixing often.
3. Stir in the lemon juice, clams juice from the cans and pepper and cook until heated completely.
4. Enjoy hot.

# Ivy League
# Muffins

🥣 Prep Time: 15 mins
🕐 Total Time: 30 mins

Servings per Recipe: 1
Calories            125.7
Fat                 3.1g
Cholesterol         27.6mg
Sodium              157.0mg
Carbohydrates       21.4g
Protein             3.0g

## Ingredients

2 1/2 C. flour
1/2 C. sugar
3 tsp baking powder
1/2 tsp salt
2 eggs, well beaten

3 tbsp butter, melted
1 C. milk
1 1/2 C. blueberries, washed and stemmed

## Directions

1. Set your oven to 375 degrees F before doing anything else and grease C. of muffin pans.
2. In a bowl, add the flour, sugar, baking powder and salt.
3. Now, sift the flour mixture into a second bowl.
4. In a third bowl, add the berries and 1/4 of the flour mixture and toss to coat well.
5. In a fourth bowl, add the milk, butter and eggs and beat until well combined.
6. Add the remaining flour mixture and mix until just combined.
7. Gently, fold in the blueberries.
8. Place the mixture into the prepared muffin C. evenly.
9. Cook in the oven for about 15-25 minutes or until a toothpick inserted in the center comes out clean.
10. Remove from the oven and keep onto the wire rack to cool in the pans for about 5 minutes.
11. Carefully, invert the muffins onto the wire rack to cool completely.
12. Enjoy.

# AUNTIE'S
# Pudding

Prep Time: 20 mins
Total Time: 1 hr 20 mins

Servings per Recipe: 6
| | |
|---|---|
| Calories | 386.0 |
| Fat | 9.6g |
| Cholesterol | 128.5mg |
| Sodium | 392.3mg |
| Carbohydrates | 64.5g |
| Protein | 11.6g |

## Ingredients

8 slices stale bread, torn
3/4 C. raisins
3 eggs, beaten
3/4 C. sugar
2 tsp vanilla

1 tsp cinnamon
1/4 tsp nutmeg
1/8 tsp salt
4 C. milk

## Directions

1. Set your oven to 350 degrees F before doing anything else.
2. In a bowl, add the raisins and top with boiling water.
3. Drain the raisins well.
4. In the bottom of an ungreased baking dish, place the bread pieces and raisins and mix well.
5. In a bowl, add the sugar, eggs, vanilla, nutmeg, cinnamon and salt and beat until well combined.
6. Add the milk and beat until well combined.
7. Place the egg mixture over the bread mixture and gently, stir to combine.
8. Arrange the baking dish into a large water filled roasting pan.
9. Cook in the oven for about 1 1/2 hours.
10. Enjoy warm.

# American
# Donuts

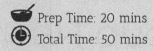 Prep Time: 20 mins

Total Time: 50 mins

Servings per Recipe: 24
| | |
|---|---|
| Calories | 124.8 |
| Fat | 2.3g |
| Cholesterol | 28.6mg |
| Sodium | 142.3mg |
| Carbohydrates | 22.8g |
| Protein | 2.8g |

## Ingredients

1 C. sour milk
4 egg yolks
2 tbsp melted shortening
1/2 tsp vanilla
4 C. flour
1 tsp salt
1/2 tsp cream of tartar

3/4 C. sugar
1/2 tsp nutmeg, grated
1 tsp cinnamon
3/4 tsp baking soda
oil

## Directions

1. In a bowl, add the flour, baking soda, cinnamon, nutmeg and salt and mix well. Now, sift the flour mixture into a second bowl.
2. In another bowl, add the egg yolks and beat until lemon colored.
3. Add the sugar and beat until well combined.
4. Add the shortening, milk, vanilla and cream of tartar and beat until well combined. Add the flour mixture and mix until a sticky dough forms. Place the dough onto a floured surface and roll into 3/4-inch thickness.
5. With a doughnut cutter, cut the doughnuts.
6. In a deep skillet, add the oil and cook until its temperature reaches to 350 degrees F.
7. Add the doughnuts in batches and cook until golden brown from both sides.
8. Add the doughnuts in batches and cook for about 2-3 minutes, flipping once half way through.
9. With a slotted spoon, transfer the doughnuts onto a paper towel-lined plate to drain.
10. Coat the warm doughnuts with the powdered sugar and enjoy.

# CHICKEN
# Soup New England

Prep Time: 25 mins
Total Time: 1 hr 40 mins

Servings per Recipe: 16
Calories         156.8
Fat              2.6g
Cholesterol      4.5mg
Sodium           253.3mg
Carbohydrates    27.4g
Protein          6.2g

## Ingredients

2 tsp olive oil
1 large Spanish onion, peeled and diced
3 cloves garlic, minced
1/2 C. celery, diced
3 C. carrots, sliced
2 parsnips, grated
4 large sweet potatoes, peeled and diced

1 1/4 C. pearl barley
2 1/2 - 3 quarts chicken stock
3 C. chicken, poached and diced
1/4 C. chopped dill
kosher salt
ground black pepper

## Directions

1. In a heavy-bottomed pan, add the oil and cook until heated through.
2. Add the carrot, celery, onions and garlic and stir for about 7 minutes.
3. Stir in the chicken, barley, parsnips and chicken and cook until boiling over medium-high heat.
4. Cook for about 28-30 minutes.
5. Stir in the sweet potatoes and cook for about 28-30 minutes.
6. Stir in the dill, salt and pepper and remove from the heat.
7. Enjoy hot.

# 6-Ingredient
# Chowder

Prep Time: 10 mins
Total Time: 30 mins

Servings per Recipe: 4
Calories            660.6
Fat                 50.1g
Cholesterol         117.7mg
Sodium              1084.0mg
Carbohydrates       39.7g
Protein             16.4g

## Ingredients

1/2-1 lb. turkey bacon, diced
1 small onion, chopped
2 C. chicken broth
2 C. cubed white potatoes

2 C. frozen corn
2 C. light cream

## Directions

1. Heat a large skillet and cook the bacon until browned completely.
2. Transfer the bacon onto a paper towel lined plate to drain and then crumble it.
3. In a 4 pan, add 2 tbsp of the bacon fat and onion over medium heat and cook for about 4-5 minutes.
4. Add the potatoes and broth and cook until boiling.
5. Cover and cook for about 10 minutes.
6. Stir in the corn and cook until heated completely.
7. Stir in the cream and cook until heated completely.
8. Enjoy with a topping of the bacon.

# COUNTRY
# Apple Cobbler

Prep Time: 15 mins

Total Time: 1 hr 10 mins

Servings per Recipe: 16

| | |
|---|---|
| Calories | 720.8 |
| Fat | 42.9 g |
| Cholesterol | 122.6mg |
| Sodium | 410.8mg |
| Carbohydrates | 81.9 g |
| Protein | 7.4g |

## Ingredients

1 1/2 C. sugar

3/4 C. chopped walnuts

1 C. flour

1 tsp baking powder

1/2 C. evaporated milk

1/2 tsp cinnamon

4 C. sliced pared apples

1/4 tsp salt

1 egg, beaten

1 C. melted butter

## Directions

1. Set your oven to 325 degrees F before doing anything else and grease an 8-inch shallow baking dish.
2. In a bowl, add 1/2 C. of the walnuts, 1/2 C. of the sugar and cinnamon and mix well.
3. In the bottom of the papered baking dish, arrange the apple slices and sprinkle with sugar the walnut mixture.
4. In a bowl, add the flour, baking powder, salt and remaining sugar and mix well.
5. In a bowl, add the butter, milk and egg and beat until well combined.
6. Add the flour mixture and mix until smooth.
7. Place the flour mixture over the apples evenly, followed by the remaining walnuts.
8. Cook in the oven for about 55 minutes.
9. Enjoy warm.

# Powwow
# Hot Pot

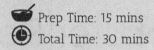 Prep Time: 15 mins
Total Time: 30 mins

Servings per Recipe: 6
Calories            567.0
Fat                 42.6g
Cholesterol         192.2mg
Sodium              431.3mg
Carbohydrates       22.2g
Protein             24.3g

## Ingredients

1/2 C. butter
1 quart oyster
1 quart whole milk
1 quart half-and-half

salt and pepper

## Directions

1. In a pan, add the oysters with their liquor and cook until the oysters starts to curl.
2. Meanwhile, in another pan, add the half-and-half and milk and cook until heated through.
3. In the pan of the oysters, add the milk mixture, salt and pepper and cook until heated completely.
4. Enjoy.

# EASY COUNTRY STYLE
# Lobster Rolls

Prep Time: 30 mins
Total Time: 30 mins

Servings per Recipe: 4
| | |
|---|---|
| Calories | 293.8 |
| Fat | 13.4g |
| Cholesterol | 7.6mg |
| Sodium | 693.4mg |
| Carbohydrates | 37.4g |
| Protein | 6.0g |

## Ingredients

1/2 C. mayonnaise
2 tsp lemon juice
1 1/2 tsp Dijon mustard
1 tsp extra virgin olive oil
1/4 tsp dried tarragon
1/4 tsp hot pepper sauce

1/4 tsp salt
1/8 tsp black pepper
2 lobster tails, cooked, shelled, and meat chopped
4 soft frankfurter rolls, split and toasted

## Directions

1. In a bowl, add the mustard, mayonnaise, olive oil, lemon juice, hot-pepper sauce, tarragon, salt and pepper and beat until well combined.
2. Add the lobster meat and mix until well combined.
3. With a plastic wrap, cover the bowl and place in the fridge for about 1 1/2-2 hours.
4. Place the lobster mixture onto each roll and enjoy.

# Vegetarian
# Bisque

Prep Time: 15 mins
Total Time: 1 hr

Servings per Recipe: 6
Calories            447.3
Fat                 27.8g
Cholesterol         74.7mg
Sodium              201.8mg
Carbohydrates       46.0g
Protein             9.1g

## Ingredients

4 tbsp salted butter
1 1/2 C. onions, diced
1 1/2 C. celery, diced
1 small fennel bulb, thinly sliced
1 tbsp chopped garlic
1 3/4 lb. zucchini, in large chunks
2 large potatoes, peeled and diced
6 C. vegetable stock
1 lb. firmly packed spinach leaves

1 C. heavy cream
1 nutmeg
salt and pepper
Leeks
4 medium leeks, sliced
2 tbsp olive oil
salt and pepper

## Directions

1. Set your oven to 450 degrees F before doing anything else.
2. In a bowl, add the oil, leeks, salt and pepper and gently, toss to coat well. In the bottom of a roasting pan, place the leek slices in a single layer. Cook in the oven for about 20 minutes, stirring twice.
3. Meanwhile, in a Dutch oven, add the butter over medium-high heat and cook until melted. Add the fennel, celery, onion and garlic and cook for about 11-12 min, stirring frequently.
4. Add the potatoes and zucchini and stir to combine.
5. Add the stock and cook until boiling. Set the heat to low and cook for about 13-15 minutes. Remove from the heat and stir in the spinach until wilted. In a food processor, add the soup mixture
6. in batches and pulse until smooth. In the same pan, add the pureed soup over medium heat. Add the cream, roasted leeks, nutmeg, salt and pepper and cook until heated completely.
7. Enjoy hot.

# PRE-COLONIAL
# Fried Clams

Prep Time: 10 mins
Total Time: 25 mins

Servings per Recipe: 2
Calories             674.5
Fat                  21.0g
Cholesterol          417.6mg
Sodium               3450.6mg
Carbohydrates        47.8g
Protein              69.9g

## Ingredients

3 C. soft shell clams, drained, and shucked
vegetable oil
3 eggs
1 C. evaporated milk
1 tsp salt

1/2 C. cornflour
lemon wedge
tartar sauce
ketchup

## Directions

1. Arrange the prepared baking sheet in the oven.
2. In a shallow bowl, add the eggs and beat well.
3. Add the milk and salt and beat until well combined.
4. In another hallow, place the flour.
5. Dip the clams into the egg mixture for at least 1 minute.
6. Then, coat the clams with the flour, shaking off any excess.
7. In a deep skillet, add about 3-inch of the vegetable oil and cook until its temperature reaches to 375 degrees F.
8. Add the clams and fry for about 1-2 minutes.
9. With a slotted spoon, transfer the clams onto a paper towel-lined plate to drain.
10. Enjoy alongside the lemon wedges, ketchup and tartar sauce.

# Lobster
# Chowder

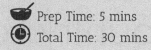

Prep Time: 5 mins
Total Time: 30 mins

Servings per Recipe: 8

| | |
|---|---|
| Calories | 511.2 |
| Fat | 25.3g |
| Cholesterol | 251.6mg |
| Sodium | 524.7mg |
| Carbohydrates | 18.8g |
| Protein | 49.8g |

## Ingredients

2 lb. white fish fillets, washed and cut into pieces
2 C. fish stock
1/2 C. butter
1/4 C. onion, chopped
1/2 C. celery, chopped
1/2 C. all-purpose flour
1 lb. clam, minced
3 C. half-and-half
2 C. red potatoes, cubed

1 bay leaf
2 tbsp parsley, chopped
1/2 lb. sea scallop, chopped
1/2 lb. shrimp, peeled, deveined, chopped
1/2 lb. lobster meat
salt
pepper
parsley

## Directions

1. In a heavy bottomed pan, add the stock and fish fillets and cook until boiling. Cook, covered for about 4-5 minutes.
2. With a slotted spoon, transfer the fish fillets into a bowl and keep aside. Transfer the stock into a bowl and reserve.
3. In the same pan, add the butter over medium heat and cook until melted completely. Add the celery and onions and stir fry for about 4-5 minutes. Stir in the flour and cook for about 4 minutes, stirring continuously. Add the reserved stock and stir to combine.
4. Add the potatoes, parsley and bay leaf and cook for about 9-10 minutes. Add the shrimp and scallops and cook until tender. Add the lobster clams and stir to combine.
5. Meanwhile, in a pan, add half-and-half over medium heat and cook until heated through. Add the hot half-and-half into the pan of the seafood mixture and cook until desired thickness, mixing frequently. Stir in the salt and pepper and remove from the heat.
6. Enjoy hot with a garnishing of the parsley.

# ROASTED
# Country Lamb

Prep Time: 25 mins
Total Time: 2 hrs 25 mins

Servings per Recipe: 6

| | |
|---|---|
| Calories | 765.4 |
| Fat | 43.1g |
| Cholesterol | 167.1mg |
| Sodium | 1028.4mg |
| Carbohydrates | 46.2g |
| Protein | 46.4g |

## Ingredients

1 tbsp vegetable oil
2 lb. boneless lean lamb, cubed
1 large onion, chopped
1/4 C. all-purpose flour
5 C. chicken broth
2 large carrots, sliced
2 large leeks, cut into pieces
2 tbsp minced fresh parsley, divided
1 bay leaf

1/2 tsp dried rosemary, crushed
1/2 tsp salt
1/4 tsp pepper
1/4 tsp dried thyme
3 large potatoes, peeled and sliced
1/4 C. butter

## Directions

1. Set your oven to 375 degrees F before doing anything else and grease a 3-quart baking dish. In a Dutch oven, add the oil and cook until heated through. Add the lamb and onion and cook for about 5-6 minutes. Stir in the flour until well combined.
2. Stir in the broth and cook until boiling, scraping the brown bits from the bottom.
3. Add the leeks, carrots, 1 tbsp of the parsley, rosemary, thyme, bay leaf, salt and pepper and stir to combine.
4. Remove from the heat and transfer the mixture into the prepared baking dish and top with the potatoes.
5. Place the butter on top in the shape of dots.
6. Cook in the oven for about 1 1/2-2 hours.
7. Remove from the oven and discard the bay leaf.
8. Enjoy with a garnishing of the remaining parsley.

# American
# Sweet Potatoes

Prep Time: 10 mins
Total Time: 35 mins

Servings per Recipe: 6
Calories          296.9
Fat               9.0g
Cholesterol       15.2mg
Sodium            145.2mg
Carbohydrates     53.4g
Protein           3.4g

## Ingredients

1 (20 oz.) can pineapple slices
1 (17 oz.) can yams, drained
1/4 C. flour
3 tbsp brown sugar
1/2 tsp cinnamon
1/8 tsp salt

3 tbsp butter
1/4 C. nuts, chopped
1 C. miniature marshmallow, optional

## Directions

1. Set your oven to 350 degrees F before doing anything else.
2. In a bowl, add the flour, cinnamon, brown sugar and salt and mix well.
3. With a pastry blender, cut in butter until a coarse crumbs like mixture forms.
4. Fold in the nuts.
5. Drain the pineapple can, reserving 1/2 C. of the juice into a bowl.
6. Arrange the pineapple slices onto the sides of a baking dish.
7. Then, arrange the yams in the center of baking dish.
8. Place the reserved pineapple juice over the yams and top with the flour mixture evenly.
9. Cook in the oven for about 25 minutes.
10. Remove the baking dish from the oven.
11. Now, set the oven to broiler.
12. Place the marshmallows on top of the yams mixture and sprinkle with the salt.
13. Cook under broiler until golden brown.

# FRIED
# Clams II

Prep Time: 20 mins
Total Time: 40 mins

Servings per Recipe: 2
| | |
|---|---|
| Calories | 407.0 |
| Fat | 12.9 g |
| Cholesterol | 206.1mg |
| Sodium | 523.2mg |
| Carbohydrates | 32.6 g |
| Protein | 37.1g |

## Ingredients

1 egg, separated
1/2 C. milk
1/4 tsp salt
1 tbsp butter, melted
1/2 C. flour, sifted

1 pint raw maine clam, shucked and drained
oil

## Directions

1. In a bowl, add the egg white and beat until stiff.
2. In another bowl, add the egg yolk, butter, milk and salt and beat until well combined.
3. Add the flour and mix well.
4. Fold in the whipped egg white.
5. Coat the clams with the mixture evenly.
6. In a deep skillet, add the oil and cook until its temperature reaches to 375 degrees F.
7. Add the clams and fry until golden brown completely.
8. With a slotted spoon, transfer the clams onto a paper towel-lined plate to drain.
9. Enjoy warm.

# *Pineapple*
# Apple Pudding

🍲 Prep Time: 30 mins
🕐 Total Time: 1 hr 30 mins

Servings per Recipe: 4
Calories               1068.4
Fat                    51.9 g
Cholesterol            197.2mg
Sodium                 54.4mg
Carbohydrates          149.0g
Protein                11.2g

## Ingredients

2 (16 oz.) cans crushed pineapple in juice, well drained
2 apples, peeled, cored and diced
3/4 C. coarsely chopped walnuts
1/2 C. packed brown sugar
2 eggs, beaten
1 C. sugar

1 C. all-purpose flour
1/4 lb. unsalted butter, plus
4 tbsp unsalted butter, melted
vanilla ice cream

## Directions

1.  Set your oven to 325 degrees F before doing anything else.
2.  In a bowl, add the apples and pineapple and mix.
3.  In a second bowl, add the brown sugar walnuts and mix well.
4.  In a third bowl, add the eggs and beat until thick.
5.  Add the flour and sugar and mix well.
6.  Add melted butter and mix until well combined.
7.  In the bottom of a 9-inch square pan, place the fruit mixture and top with the walnut mixture, followed by the flour mixture.
8.  Cook in the oven for about 1 hour.
9.  Enjoy warm with a topping of the vanilla ice cream.

# DARK RYE
# Bread

Prep Time: 20 mins
Total Time: 2 hrs 20 mins

Servings per Recipe: 12
| | |
|---|---|
| Calories | 193.7 |
| Fat | 2.6g |
| Cholesterol | 21.1mg |
| Sodium | 239.6mg |
| Carbohydrates | 40.1g |
| Protein | 4.3g |

## Ingredients

1 C. rye flour
1 1/2 C. cornmeal
1 tsp baking soda
1/2 tsp salt
1/2 C. dark molasses, warmed

2 C. milk
1 egg, beaten
1 C. raisins

## Directions

1. In a bowl, add the cornmeal, rye flour, baking soda and salt and mix well.
2. In another bowl, add the egg. milk and molasses and mix until well combined.
3. Adding the flour mixture and mix until well combined.
4. Fold in the raisins.
5. Divide the mixture into greased 2 (1-lb.) coffee cans evenly.
6. With 1 foil piece, cover each can tightly with foil and then, seal with string.
7. In a pan, add about 2-inch of the water.
8. Carefully, arrange the cans in the pan.
9. With a lid of the foil, cover the pan tightly.
10. Place the pan over high heat and cook until boiling.
11. Set the heat to low and cook for about 2 hours, checking often to keep 1-inch of water in the pan.
12. Remove from the heat and transfer the cans onto wire racks.
13. Carefully, remove the foil and keep aside to cool for about 20 minutes.
14. Carefully, invert each bread onto plates and enjoy.

# *Boston*
# Baked Beans III

🥣 Prep Time: 1 hr
🕐 Total Time: 5 hrs

Servings per Recipe: 6
Calories            583.8
Fat                 9.9g
Cholesterol         12.8mg
Sodium              792.8mg
Carbohydrates       107.8g
Protein             19.8g

## Ingredients

1 lb. dried navy beans, soaked overnight and drained
1/4 lb. turkey bacon, uncooked, cut into pieces
1/2 C. onion, chopped
1 C. brown sugar
1/2 C. ketchup

1/4 C. molasses
1/4 C. maple syrup
2 tsp dried mustard
1 tsp salt
3 C. water

## Directions

1.  In a pan of the water, cook the beans until desired doneness.
2.  Meanwhile, set your oven to 250 degrees F.
3.  In another pan, add the brown sugar, ketchup, molasses, maple syrup, mustard, salt and water and cook until boiling, stirring frequently.
4.  Drain the beans well and transfer into a bean pot.
5.  Add the molasses mixture, bacon and onion and stir to combine.
6.  Cover the pot and cook in the oven for about 4 hours, check occasionally to keep the liquid proper.
7.  Enjoy hot.

# DARK MOLASSES
# Cookies

Prep Time: 10 mins
Total Time: 25 mins

Servings per Recipe: 1
| | |
|---|---|
| Calories | 115.5 |
| Fat | 4.5g |
| Cholesterol | 7.7mg |
| Sodium | 80.4mg |
| Carbohydrates | 17.4g |
| Protein | 1.3g |

## Ingredients

1 C. plus 1/4 C. sugar
1 C. shortening
1 C. dark molasses
2 eggs
4 C. sifted all-purpose flour

1 tsp baking soda
1 tsp salt
2 tsp cinnamon
1 tsp ginger

## Directions

1. Set your oven to 350 degrees F before doing anything else and lightly, grease a cookie sheet.
2. In a bowl, add the flour, baking soda, cinnamon, ginger and salt and mix well.
3. Now, sift the flour mixture into a second bowl.
4. In another bowl, add the shortening and 1 C. of the sugar and beat until creamy.
5. Add the eggs and molasses and beat until well combined.
6. Add the flour mixture and mix until well combined.
7. In a separate bowl, place about 1/4 C. of the sugar.
8. With the sugar coated fingers, make about 1-1/2-inch balls from the dough.
9. In the bottom of the prepared cookie sheet, arrange the dough balls about 3-inch apart.
10. Cook in the oven for about 12-15 minutes.
11. Remove from the oven and keep onto the wire rack to cool in the pan for about 5 minutes.
12. Carefully, invert the cookies onto the wire rack to cool completely.
13. Enjoy.

# Autumn
# Bisque

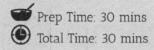 Prep Time: 30 mins

Total Time: 30 mins

Servings per Recipe: 12
Calories          289.3
Fat               15.8g
Cholesterol       46.7mg
Sodium            363.3mg
Carbohydrates     31.1g
Protein           7.1g

## Ingredients

1/4 lb. butter
1 medium onion, dice
1 - 2 red pears, peeled seeded and chopped
2 tbsp sage leaves, chopped
3/4 C. flour
2 1/2 quarts chicken stock

2 (15 oz.) cans solid pack pumpkin
1/2 C. brown sugar
3 tsp curry powder
3/4 C. heavy cream

## Directions

1. In a heavy-bottomed pot, add the butter and cook until melted.
2. Add the pears and onions and stir fry about 5 minutes.
3. Add the sage, salt and pepper and stir to combine.
4. Add the flour and cook for about 1-2 minutes, mixing continuously.
5. Gradually, add the stock slowly, beating continuously until smooth.
6. Add the pumpkin, brown sugar and curry powder and cook until boiling.
7. Cook for about 30 minutes.
8. With an immersion blender, blend the soup until pureed.
9. Stir in the cream and cook until heated completely.
10. Enjoy hot.

# 30-MINUTE
# Shrimp Chowder

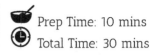

Prep Time: 10 mins
Total Time: 30 mins

Servings per Recipe: 6
| | |
|---|---|
| Calories | 164.7 |
| Fat | 3.2g |
| Cholesterol | 73.0mg |
| Sodium | 377.8mg |
| Carbohydrates | 20.8g |
| Protein | 13.2g |

## Ingredients

1 (10 oz.) boxes frozen corn in butter sauce, thawed
1 tbsp olive oil
1 medium onion, chopped
1 medium bell pepper, chopped
1 stalk celery, chopped
2 garlic cloves, chopped
1 C. reduced-sodium chicken broth
1 large potato, peeled, cubed

1/4 tsp dried thyme leaves
1/8 tsp ground red pepper
2 tbsp all-purpose flour
2 C. nonfat milk, skim
12 oz. shrimp, cooked peeled and deveined tails removed

## Directions

1. In a pot, add the oil over medium heat and cook until heated through.
2. Add the celery, bell pepper, onion and garlic and stir fry for about 4-5 minutes.
3. Add the potato, thyme, red pepper and broth and bring to a boil.
4. Set the heat and cook, covered for about 8-10 minutes.
5. Stir in the corn and bring to a boil, mixing frequently.
6. Meanwhile, in a bowl, add the flour and milk and beat until smooth.
7. Add the flour mixture into the pot, stirring continuously and bring to a boil.
8. Set the heat to low and cook for about 5 minutes.
9. Stir in the shrimp and cook for about 2 minutes.
10. Enjoy hot.

# Artisanal
# Pudding

🥣 Prep Time: 15 mins
🕐 Total Time: 1 hr

Servings per Recipe: 6
Calories            355.8
Fat                 16.5g
Cholesterol         160.7mg
Sodium              671.5mg
Carbohydrates       42.4g
Protein             11.5g

## Ingredients

2 C. whole kernel corn
8 tbsp flour
8 tbsp sugar
4 whole eggs
1 tsp salt

1 quart whole milk
4 tbsp sweet butter, melted

## Directions

1. Set your oven to 450 degrees F before doing anything else and grease a baking dish.
2. In a bowl, add the corn, butter, flour, sugar and salt and mix until well combined.
3. In another bowl, add the eggs and beat lightly.
4. Add the milk and mix well.
5. Add the milk mixture into the corn mixture and mix well.
6. In the bottom of the prepared baking dish, place the mixture evenly.
7. Cook in the oven for about 45 minutes, stirring with a fork, 3 times.
8. Enjoy warm.

# NORTHERN
# Black Eyed Dinner

Prep Time: 1 hr
Total Time: 12 hrs

Servings per Recipe: 5
| | |
|---|---|
| Calories | 1121.4 |
| Fat | 56.0g |
| Cholesterol | 189.7mg |
| Sodium | 953.1mg |
| Carbohydrates | 77.1g |
| Protein | 76.9g |

## Ingredients

1 (16 oz.) packages dried black-eyed peas, rinsed/picked over
1 (11 1/2 oz.) cans bean with bacon soup
3 C. hot water
3 medium carrots, chopped
2 medium onions, sliced
1 tsp garlic powder
1/2 tsp seasoning salt

3 lb. boneless beef chuck roast, trimmed of fat in chunks
1 tsp hickory liquid smoke
1 (4 oz.) cans diced green chilies
1 red bell pepper, chopped

## Directions

1. In a slow cooker, add the beans, onions, carrots, hot water, undiluted soup, garlic powder and seasoned salt and mix well.
2. Arrange the roast over beans mixture and
3. press into the mixture.
4. Set the slow cooker on Low and cook, covered for about 9-10 hours.
5. Now, set the slow cooker on High.
6. Stir in the bell pepper, chilies and liquid smoke and cook, uncovered for about 12-15 minutes.
7. With a slotted spoon, remove any fat from the top and enjoy.

# *Kennebec*
# Cake

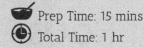 Prep Time: 15 mins
Total Time: 1 hr

Servings per Recipe: 8
Calories          356.3
Fat               17.8g
Cholesterol       103.4mg
Sodium            312.9mg
Carbohydrates     43.2g
Protein           6.7g

## Ingredients

2 C. milk
4 tsp white vinegar
1 C. all-purpose flour
3/4 C. yellow cornmeal, preferably stone-ground
3/4 C. sugar
1/2 tsp baking soda

1/2 tsp salt
2 large eggs
2 tbsp butter
1 C. heavy cream

## Directions

1.  Set your oven to 350 degrees F before doing anything else.
2.  In a bowl, add the milk and vinegar and stir to combine.
3.  Keep aside until milk becomes sour.
4.  In a second bowl, add the cornmeal, flour, sugar, baking soda and salt and mix well.
5.  Add the eggs into the bowl of the sour milk and beat well.
6.  Add the flour mixture and mix until just combined.
7.  In a 12-inch cast-iron skillet, add the butter and cook until melted.
8.  Place the mixture over the butter evenly and then, put the cream in the center.
9.  Transfer the skillet into the oven and cook for about 45 minutes.
10. Remove from the oven and keep aside to cool slightly.
11. Cut into desired sized wedges and enjoy warm.

# MY FIRST
# Pot Roast

Prep Time: 15 mins
Total Time: 8 hrs 15 mins

Servings per Recipe: 4

| | |
|---|---|
| Calories | 1212.6 |
| Fat | 67.7g |
| Cholesterol | 234.7mg |
| Sodium | 1068.3mg |
| Carbohydrates | 77.7g |
| Protein | 70.9g |

## Ingredients

3 - 4 lb. beef roast
8 small red potatoes, quartered
8 medium carrots, cut into chunks
1 small onion, chopped
1 (8 oz.) jars prepared horseradish
1 - 2 tsp salt

1/4 - 1/2 tsp black pepper
1 C. water
2 tbsp cornstarch
2 tbsp water

## Directions

1. In a bowl, add the horseradish, 1 C. of the water, salt and pepper and mix well.
2. In a slow cooker, place the carrots, potatoes and onion and top with the beef, followed by the horseradish mixture.
3. Set the slow cooker on Low and cook, covered for about 8-10 hours.
4. Meanwhile, in a bowl, dissolve the cornstarch into 2 tbsp of the cold water.
5. Uncover the slow cooker and transfer 2 C. of the pan juices into a pan.
6. Stir in the cornstarch mixture and cook until desired thickness, mixing continuously.
7. Enjoy the beef and vegetables alongside the gravy.

# Hot Potato
# Chowder

Prep Time: 20 mins
Total Time: 1 hr 40 mins

Servings per Recipe: 4
| | |
|---|---|
| Calories | 377.2 |
| Fat | 12.5g |
| Cholesterol | 53.3mg |
| Sodium | 1302.8mg |
| Carbohydrates | 51.2g |
| Protein | 20.4g |

## Ingredients

6 oz. smoked turkey breast, diced
1 medium onion, diced
2 stalks celery, diced
1 large potato, diced
4 C. chicken broth
1/4 C. green chili, mild, chopped, canned
1 lb. corn

1/2 C. cream
salt and pepper

## Directions

1. In a pan, add all the ingredients except the cream and cook until boiling.
2. Set the heat to low and cook for about 1 hour.
3. Stir in the cream and cook for about 18-20 minutes, mixing occasionally.
4. Enjoy warm.

# WATERBURY
# Chicken Hot Pot

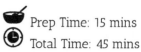
Prep Time: 15 mins
Total Time: 45 mins

Servings per Recipe: 6
Calories            579.8
Fat                 38.9g
Cholesterol         199.0mg
Sodium              287.1mg
Carbohydrates       21.2g
Protein             36.3g

## Ingredients

2 tbsp olive oil
2 lb. chicken breasts, cut into pieces
1 beaten egg, with
1/2 tsp hot pepper sauce
seasoning salt
flour
2 ripe pears, pared, cored, cut into
wedges
1 granny smith apple, pared, cored, cut
into wedges
2 tbsp butter

2 celery ribs, chopped
2 large onions, diced
2 C. chicken stock
2/3 C. apple cider, reduced
1 C. heavy cream
1/2 tsp vanilla extract
1/3 C. toasted chopped hazelnuts
2 chopped scallions

## Directions

1. For reduced apple cider: in a pan, add 2 C. of the apple cider and boil until reduces to half. In 2 separate shallow dishes, place the egg mixture and seasoned flour respectively. Dip the chicken pieces into the egg mixture and then, coat with the seasoned flour.

2. In a skillet, add the oil over medium-high heat and cook until heated through. Add the chicken pieces and cook until browned completely. With a slotted spoon, transfer the chicken pieces onto a plate. In the same skillet, add the pear and apple pieces and stir fry for about 3 minutes. With a slotted spoon, transfer the fruit pieces into a bowl. In the same skillet, add the butter and cook until melted. Add the onion and celery and stir fry for about 4-5 minutes.

3. Add the cooked chicken, broth and 2/3 C. of the apple cider and cook until boiling. Set the heat to low and cook, covered for about 18-20 minutes. Stir in the fruit pieces with any juices and cook until heated completely.

4. Enjoy hot with a topping of the scallion and hazelnuts.

# How to Make
# Chop Suey

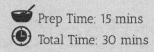 Prep Time: 15 mins

Total Time: 30 mins

Servings per Recipe: 8
| | |
|---|---|
| Calories | 436.5 |
| Fat | 10.3g |
| Cholesterol | 38.5mg |
| Sodium | 891.8mg |
| Carbohydrates | 64.9g |
| Protein | 22.8g |

## Ingredients

1 medium yellow onion, chopped
3 large garlic cloves, minced
1 lb. ground beef
1 lb. elbow macaroni
1 tsp dried parsley
1/2 tbsp kosher salt
1/2 tsp black pepper

1/2 tsp cayenne pepper
1 (28 oz.) cans Italian-style crushed tomatoes
2 (10 oz.) cans condensed tomato soup
10 oz. water
1 tsp sugar
8 baby portabella mushrooms, sliced

## Directions

1. In the pan of the water, add a splash of the oil, oregano and salt and cook until boiling. Add the elbow macaroni and cook for about 9-10 minutes. Drain the pasta and return to pan.

2. In a skillet, 1/2 tbsp of the oil over medium heat and cook until heated.

3. Add the onion and cook for about 4-5 minutes.

4. Add the beef and cook until browned completely.

5. Add the mushrooms and garlic and cook for about 2 minutes.

6. Remove the excess grease from the skillet.

7. Transfer the beef mixture into the pan with the pasta over low heat.

8. Add the condensed tomato soup, tomatoes and 1 soup can filled water worth of water and cook for about 12-15 minutes.

9. Stir in the sugar, cayenne pepper, salt and black pepper and remove from the heat.

10. Enjoy hot.

# EASY
# Coffee Cakes

🥣 Prep Time: 30 mins
🕐 Total Time:1 hr 25 mins

Servings per Recipe: 8
Calories           263.1
Fat                8.5g
Cholesterol        28.5mg
Sodium             194.2mg
Carbohydrates      43.0g
Protein            5.7g

## Ingredients

1 1/2 C. whole wheat flour, sifted
1/2 C. white flour, sifted
1 C. frozen cranberries
2/3 C. granulated sugar
1/2 C. chopped walnuts
2 tsp baking powder
1 tsp grated orange peel
1/2 tsp baking soda

1/2 C. milk
1/3 C. orange juice
1/4 C. canola oil
2 tbsp unsweetened applesauce
1 egg
1 egg white

## Directions

1. Set your oven to 375 degrees F before doing anything else and grease a 9x5-inch loaf pan.
2. In a bowl, add the flours, walnuts, cranberries, orange peel, sugar, baking powder and baking soda and mix until well combined.
3. In another bowl, add the egg, egg white, applesauce, oil, milk and orange juice and beat until well combined.
4. Add the flour mixture and mix until just combined.
5. Place the mixture into the prepared loaf pan evenly.
6. Cook in the oven for about 55 minutes or until a toothpick inserted in the center comes out clean.
7. Remove from the oven and keep onto the wire rack to cool in the pan for about 10-15 minutes.
8. Carefully, invert the cake onto the wire rack to cool completely.
9. Cut into desired sized slices and enjoy.

# Citrus
# Mint Morning Tea

Prep Time: 5 mins
Total Time: 15 mins

Servings per Recipe: 12

| | |
|---|---|
| Calories | 73.6 |
| Fat | 0.0g |
| Cholesterol | 0.0mg |
| Sodium | 3.8mg |
| Carbohydrates | 19.0g |
| Protein | 0.1g |

## Ingredients

1 C. water
1 C. sugar
2 tsp black tea
1/4 tsp dried mint
1/2 tsp allspice
6 tbsp lemon juice
3/4 C. orange juice

2 quarts water, boiling

## Directions

1. In a pan, add the sugar and water and boil for about 4-5 minutes.
2. Stir in the mint, tea and allspice and immediately, cover the pan.
3. Remove from the heat and keep aside, covered to steep for about 10 minutes.
4. Through a trainer, strain the tea into a pan.
5. Add the boiling water, lemon and orange juice and cook until boiling.
6. Enjoy hot.

# SALEM
# Hot Dog Puffs

Prep Time: 10 mins
Total Time: 20 mins

Servings per Recipe: 6
| | |
|---|---|
| Calories | 328.0 |
| Fat | 19.2g |
| Cholesterol | 34.0mg |
| Sodium | 868.1mg |
| Carbohydrates | 28.7g |
| Protein | 10.2g |

## Ingredients

6 beef hot dogs
2 tbsp butter, divided in half
6 hot dog buns
2 tbsp sweet relish
2 tbsp ketchup
2 tbsp yellow mustard

2 tbsp cider vinegar
1 lb. napa cabbage, shredded & chopped
salt and pepper

## Directions

1. In a bowl, add the mustard, ketchup, relish and vinegar and mix until well combined.
2. Add the cabbage, salt and pepper and mix until well combined.
3. With a fork, pierce the casing pf hot dogs.
4. In a skillet, add hot dogs and 1-inch of water and cook until boiling.
5. Cook for about 5-7 minutes.
6. Drain the hot dogs completely.
7. In the same skillet, add 1 tbsp of the butter over medium heat and cook until melted.
8. Add the hot dogs and cook until browned completely.
9. Transfer the hot dogs into a bowl.
10. With paper towels, wipe out the skillet.
11. In the same skillet, add the remaining butter and cook until melted.
12. Add the rolls and cook until golden brown.
13. Place the hot dogs in each roll and top with the cabbage slaw.
14. Enjoy.

# 5-Ingredient
# Fish Cakes

Prep Time: 30 mins
Total Time: 2 hrs 30 mins

Servings per Recipe: 8
| | |
|---|---|
| Calories | 270.3 |
| Fat | 2.6g |
| Cholesterol | 132.8mg |
| Sodium | 4015.9mg |
| Carbohydrates | 20.0g |
| Protein | 39.5g |

## Ingredients

1 lb. salt cod fish
2 lb. potatoes
2 eggs, well beaten with

1/2 tsp fresh ground black pepper
butter

## Directions

1. In a bowl, soak the cod into cold water and keep aside for about 1 1/2-2 hours, changing the water twice.
2. Now, tear the cod into pieces.
3. Cut the edges of the potatoes.
4. In a pan of the water, add the cod and cook until potatoes are tender.
5. Drain well and transfer the cod and potatoes in separate bowls separately.
6. With a fork, mash the potatoes.
7. Carefully, shred the cod, removing any bones.
8. In the bowl, add the cod, potatoes, egg mixture and salt and mix well.
9. Make 1/2-inch thick patties from the mixture.
10. In a heavy skillet, add the butter over medium heat and cook until melted.
11. Add the patties and cook for about 4-6 minutes, flipping once half way through.
12. Enjoy hot.

# PORTSMOUTH
# Deli Crab Melts

Prep Time: 15 mins
Total Time: 25 mins

Servings per Recipe: 4
| | |
|---|---|
| Calories | 539.7 |
| Fat | 29.7g |
| Cholesterol | 76.3mg |
| Sodium | 1162.9mg |
| Carbohydrates | 36.7g |
| Protein | 32.1g |

## Ingredients

3 jarred roasted red peppers, drained
salt
pepper
1 lemon, juice
3 tbsp olive oil
12 oz. imitation crab meat
2 tsp Old Bay Seasoning
2 celery ribs, chopped
2 sprigs tarragon, leaves stripped from

the stems and chopped
3 scallions, chopped
4 English muffins, split
unsalted butter, softened
2 C. watercress, chopped
2 C. shredded Gruyere cheese

## Directions

1. Set the broiler of your oven.
2. In a blender, add the peppers, lemon juice, hot sauce, salt and pepper and pulse until combined.
3. While the motor is running, add the olive oil and pulse until smooth.
4. In a bowl, add the crab, pepper dressing, celery, scallions, tarragon and seafood seasoning. and mix until well combined.
5. Cook under the broiler until toasted lightly.
6. Remove them from muffins from the oven and keep aside.
7. Place the butter onto each muffin half evenly, followed by the watercress, crab salad and cheese.
8. Cook the open face sandwiches under the broiler for about 1-2 minutes.
9. Enjoy hot.

# *Classical*
# Baked Beans from Boston

Prep Time: 30 mins
Total Time: 3 hrs

Servings per Recipe: 6
Calories             390.1
Fat                  1.3g
Cholesterol          0.0mg
Sodium               461.6mg
Carbohydrates        80.1g
Protein              17.3g

## Ingredients

1 lb. dried navy beans, discarded
discolored beans, soaked overnight and
drained
1 large onion, coarse chop
2 tbsp Dijon mustard
1/4 C. dark brown sugar

1/3 C. light brown sugar
1/4 C. molasses
1 tsp salt

## Directions

1. In a pan, add the beans with enough water to cover by 1-inch and cook until boiling.

2. Set the heat to low and simmer for about 43-45 minutes.

3. Drain the beans, reserving the cooking water into a bowl.

4. Set your oven to 325 degrees F.

5. In a bean pot, add the beans, mustard, onion, molasses, both brown sugars, salt with enough of the reserved cooking water to just cover the mixture and stir to combine.

6. Place the pot over high heat and cook until boiling.

7. Remove from the heat and immediately, transfer into the oven.

8. Cover the pot with the lid and cook in the oven for about 2 hours, checking after every 30 minutes.

9. Remove the lid and cook for about 20-30 minutes.

10. Enjoy hot.

# BRENDA'S
# Tuna Melts

Prep Time: 30 mins
Total Time: 40 mins

Servings per Recipe: 4
| | |
|---|---|
| Calories | 673.7 |
| Fat | 42.2g |
| Cholesterol | 153.2mg |
| Sodium | 1415.5mg |
| Carbohydrates | 19.2g |
| Protein | 53.9g |

## Ingredients

4 sandwich-size sourdough English muffins, halved horizontally
2 (9 oz.) cans tuna in water, well-drained
5 tbsp sweet pickle relish
1/2 medium white onion, chopped
2 stalks celery & leaves, chopped
2 tsp Old Bay Seasoning
1/2 C. mayonnaise

4 radishes, chopped
salt
black pepper
2 vine-ripened tomatoes, sliced
3/4-1 lb. sharp white cheddar cheese, sliced

## Directions

1. Set the broiler of your oven.
2. Arrange the muffin halves onto a baking sheet, cut side up.
3. Cook under the broiler until toasted lightly.
4. Remove them from muffins from the oven but leave the broiler on.
5. In a bowl, add the relish, mayonnaise, tuna, celery, onion, radishes, Old Bay seasoning, salt and pepper and with 2 forks, mash until well combined.
6. Place the tuna mixture top of the each muffin half evenly, followed by the tomato and cheese slices.
7. Cook the open face sandwiches under the broiler until the cheese is melted.
8. Enjoy hot.

# *Newport*
# Scallop Platter

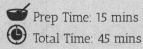
Prep Time: 15 mins
Total Time: 45 mins

Servings per Recipe: 8
Calories            440.6
Fat                 25.4g
Cholesterol         139.1mg
Sodium              502.5mg
Carbohydrates       27.6g
Protein             24.7g

## Ingredients

1/2 C. butter, melted
2 C. breadcrumbs
1 quart oyster, shucked
1 tbsp celery seed
salt and pepper
1 C. cream

1 pint scallops

## Directions

1. Set your oven to 400 degrees F before doing anything else and grease a baking dish.
2. In a bowl, add the breadcrumbs and butter and mix well.
3. In the bottom of the prepared baking dish, spread 1/3 of the breadcrumbs mixture.
4. Place the half of the oysters on top, followed by half of the seasonings, some of the cream, half of the scallops, seasonings, 1/3 of the breadcrumbs mixture, remaining oysters, cream, scallops and remaining breadcrumbs mixture.
5. Cook in the oven for about 30 minutes.
6. Enjoy hot.

# AMERICAN
# Cheese Pops

Prep Time: 15 mins
Total Time: 20 mins

Servings per Recipe: 6
| | |
|---|---|
| Calories | 113.7 |
| Fat | 2.5g |
| Cholesterol | 64.8mg |
| Sodium | 288.4mg |
| Carbohydrates | 17.2g |
| Protein | 4.9g |

## Ingredients

1 C. flour
1 tsp baking powder
1/2 tsp salt
1/4 tsp paprika
1/4 tsp dry mustard

2 eggs, separated
1/2 C. milk
1 C. American cheese, grated
oil

## Directions

1. In a bowl, add the flour, baking powder, mustard, paprika and salt and mix well.
2. Now, sift the flour mixture into a second bowl.
3. In another bowl, add the egg yolks and beat well.
4. Add the milk and stir to combine.
5. add the flour mixture and mix until well combined.
6. Add the cheese and stir to combine.
7. In a glass bowl, add the egg whites and beat until stiff peaks form.
8. Gently, fold the whipped egg whites into the flour mixture.
9. In a deep skillet, add the oil and cook until its temperature reaches to 360 degrees F.
10. With a spoon, add the mixture and cook until golden brown completely.
11. With a slotted spoon, transfer the puffs onto a paper towel-lined plate to drain.
12. Enjoy.

# Country Style
# Squash

Prep Time: 15 mins
Total Time: 30 mins

Servings per Recipe: 5
| | |
|---|---|
| Calories | 297.1 |
| Fat | 11.9g |
| Cholesterol | 24.4mg |
| Sodium | 81.0mg |
| Carbohydrates | 53.2g |
| Protein | 3.3g |

## Ingredients

1 medium butternut squash, halved
lengthwise and seeded
1/4 C. butter, melted
1/4 C. maple syrup

3/4 C. ground cinnamon
1/4 C. ground nutmeg

## Directions

1. In a microwave-safe dish, place the squash halves, cut side down.
2. Add about 1/2-inch of the water in the dish.
3. Cover the dish and microwave on High for about 18-20 minutes.
4. Drain the squash halves completely and keep aside to cool slightly.
5. With a spoon, scoop out the pulp and transfer into a bowl.
6. With a potato masher, mash the pulp.
7. Add the maple syrup, butter, nutmeg and cinnamon and mix well.
8. Enjoy.

# AMERICAN
# Blueberry Pie

Prep Time: 10 mins
Total Time: 25 mins

Servings per Recipe: 6
| | |
|---|---|
| Calories | 508.4 |
| Fat | 26.9g |
| Cholesterol | 59.4mg |
| Sodium | 289.7mg |
| Carbohydrates | 66.2g |
| Protein | 3.7g |

## Ingredients

4 C. blueberries
1/2 C. granulated sugar
1/2 C. light brown sugar
2 1/2 tbsp flour
1 tbsp butter
1 tbsp lemon juice
1/4 tsp allspice
1/4 tsp cinnamon

1/8 tsp nutmeg
1/4 tsp salt
1 pie shell, baked
1 C. whipping cream
1/2 tsp vanilla
sugar

## Directions

1. In a pot, add the butter, 2 C. of the blueberries, flour, sugars, lemon juice, spices and salt over low heat and cook until just boiling.
2. Set the heat to low and cook for about 5 minutes, mixing continuously.
3. Add the remaining blueberries and stir to combine.
4. Place the mixture into the baked pie shell evenly.
5. Refrigerate to chill completely.
6. Enjoy with a topping of the whipped cream.

# *Vermont*
# Autumn Muffins

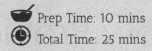 Prep Time: 10 mins

Total Time: 25 mins

Servings per Recipe: 1

| | |
|---|---|
| Calories | 1563.4 |
| Fat | 105.5g |
| Cholesterol | 303.6mg |
| Sodium | 1899.7mg |
| Carbohydrates | 134.8g |
| Protein | 24.4g |

## Ingredients

2 C. all-purpose flour
2 tsp baking powder
1 1/4 tsp baking soda
1/4 tsp salt
1/2 C. butter, softened
1/4 C. pure maple syrup

1 1/2 C. sour cream
1 large egg
1/2 C. pecans, chopped

## Directions

1. Set your oven to 375 degrees F before doing anything else and line 12 cups of a muffin pan with the paper liners.
2. In a bowl, add the flour, baking soda, baking powder and salt and mix well.
3. In another bowl, add the butter and with an electric mixer, beat on medium speed until fluffy and light.
4. Gradually, add the maple syrup and beat until well combined.
5. Add the egg and sour cream and beat until well combined.
6. Add the flour mixture, 1/2 C. at a time and beat on low speed until just combined.
7. Gently, fold in the pecans.
8. the mixture into the prepared muffin cups about 2/3 of the full.
9. Cook in the oven for about 15-20 minutes.
10. Remove from the oven and keep onto the wire rack to cool in the pan for about 5 minutes.
11. Carefully, invert the muffins onto the wire rack to cool completely.
12. Enjoy.

# CHILI
# New Providence

Prep Time: 20 mins
Total Time: 4 hrs 40 mins

Servings per Recipe: 8

| | |
|---|---|
| Calories | 408.3 |
| Fat | 15.7g |
| Cholesterol | 0.0mg |
| Sodium | 1951.9mg |
| Carbohydrates | 55.1g |
| Protein | 15.6g |

## Ingredients

1/2 C. dried great northern beans, soaked and drained

1/2 C. dried red kidney beans, soaked and drained

1/2 C. dried black-eyed peas, soaked and drained

1/2 C. dried black beans, soaked and drained

1/2 C. olive oil

3 tbsp minced garlic

2 1/2 C. onions, diced

2 C. carrots, diced

1 C. yellow pepper, diced

1 C. sweet red pepper, diced

1 C. green pepper, diced

3 C. canned diced tomatoes

2 C. v 8 vegetable juice

1 C. vegetable stock

1 1/2 tbsp chili powder

1 1/2 tbsp cumin

1 tbsp oregano

1 tbsp basil

3 bay leaves

2 tbsp kosher salt

1 tsp pepper

2 tbsp Tabasco sauce

2 tbsp balsamic vinegar

## Directions

1. In a pan of the water, add all the beans and cook until boiling.
2. Cook for about 2 1/2-3 hours. Drain the beans and keep aside to cool. In the same pan, add the oil and cook until heated through.
3. Add the peppers, carrots, onions and garlic and cook for about 8-10 minutes. Add the tomatoes, beans, V-8, basil, oregano, bay leaves, cumin and chili powder and stir to combine.
4. Set the heat to low and cook, covered for about 1 hour.
5. Stir in the Tabasco sauce, vinegar, salt and pepper and remove from the heat.
6. Enjoy hot.

# Mashed Potato
# Alternative
# (Creamy Turnips)

Prep Time: 6 mins
Total Time: 27 mins

Servings per Recipe: 4
| | |
|---|---|
| Calories | 92.8 |
| Fat | 6.7g |
| Cholesterol | 18.0mg |
| Sodium | 565.8mg |
| Carbohydrates | 7.7g |
| Protein | 1.3g |

## Ingredients

1 lb. turnip, peeled and cubed
1/2 tsp salt
2 tbsp butter
2 tbsp half-and-half

1/4 tsp salt
1/4 tsp pepper

## Directions

1. In a pan of the boiling water, add the turnip and 1/2 tsp of the salt and cook until boiling.
2. Set the heat to low and cook, covered for about 18-20 minutes.
3. Drain the turnips completely and return into the same pan over low heat
4. Cook for about 1 minute and remove from the heat.
5. Immediately, add the half-and-half, butter, remaining salt and pepper and with a potato masher, mash until soft and fluffy.
6. Enjoy hot.

# WHITE BEAN
# Casserole

Prep Time: 25 mins
Total Time: 1 hr 25 mins

Servings per Recipe: 8
Calories              330.3
Fat                   6.5g
Cholesterol           15.2mg
Sodium                517.8mg
Carbohydrates         59.8g
Protein               11.6g

## Ingredients

1 (48 oz.) jars great northern beans,
drained
4 tbsp butter
3 C. cubed tart cooking apples
1/2 C. chopped onion
3/4 C. light brown sugar
1/2 C. catsup

1 tsp cinnamon
1 tsp salt
1 tsp fresh ground black pepper

## Directions

1.  Set your oven to 375 degrees F before doing anything else.
2.  In a skillet, add the butter and cook until melted.
3.  Add the onions and apples and cook for about 8-10 minutes.
4.  Add the brown sugar and cook until dissolved, mixing continuously.
5.  Add the catsup, cinnamon, salt and pepper and stir to combine.
6.  In the bottom of a casserole dish, place the beans and apple mixture and stir to combine well.
7.  Cook in the oven for about 1 hour.
8.  Enjoy hot.

# *Dinner Rolls*
# New England Style

Prep Time: 3 hrs
Total Time: 3 hrs 30 mins

Servings per Recipe: 1
| | |
|---|---|
| Calories | 137.8 |
| Fat | 1.5g |
| Cholesterol | 3.4mg |
| Sodium | 86.3mg |
| Carbohydrates | 26.9g |
| Protein | 3.7g |

## Ingredients

1 large potato, peeled, cubed, cooked and mashed
3/4 C. potato water
1/2 tsp salt
2 tbsp sugar
1 1/2 tbsp butter
4 tbsp lukewarm milk

1 (1 tbsp) package active dry yeast
3 1/2 C. flour

## Directions

1. In a bowl, add the yeast, 1 tbsp of the sugar and 1/4 C. of the warm potato water and mix until well combined.
2. In a bowl, add the potatoes and mash well.
3. Add the butter, milk, reserved potato water, 1 tbsp of the sugar and salt and mix until well combined. Add the yeast mixture and stir to combine.
4. Add 2 C. of the flour and beat until well combined.
5. Add the remaining flour and mix until just firm dough forms.
6. Now, with your hands, knead the dough until smooth.
7. In a bowl, add the dough and coat the top with some oil.
8. With a plastic wrap, cover the bowl and keep aside until doubled in size. Transfer the dough onto a floured surface and pat into 1/2-inch thickness.
9. Make 16-20 rolls from the dough and arrange into a greased baking dish.
10. Keep aside for about 35-45 minutes.
11. Set your oven to 400 degree F.
12. Cook the rolls in the oven for about 20 minutes.
13. Enjoy warm.

# BOSTON
# Chicken McMuffins

 Prep Time: 30 mins
Total Time: 42 mins

Servings per Recipe: 4
| | |
|---|---|
| Calories | 399.7 |
| Fat | 27.3g |
| Cholesterol | 130.0mg |
| Sodium | 232.4mg |
| Carbohydrates | 12.7g |
| Protein | 27.1g |

## Ingredients

1 1/3 lb. ground chicken
salt
black pepper
1 tsp poultry seasoning
4 tbsp extra virgin olive oil
1 small red onion, sliced
1 granny smith apple, quartered, cored, and sliced

4 sandwich-size English muffins, split and toasted
8 slices sharp aged cheddar cheese
4 tbsp honey mustard
1 1/2 C. watercress, chopped
specialty potato chips

## Directions

1. Set the broiler of your oven. In a bowl, add the chicken, poultry seasoning, salt and pepper and mix well. Make 4 thin patties from the mixture. In a skillet, add 2 tbsp of the oil over medium-high heat and cook until heated through. Add the chicken patties and cook for about 10 minutes, flipping once half way through.

2. Meanwhile, in another skillet, add 2 tbsp of the oil over medium-high heat and cook until heated through.

3. Add the apples, onions, salt and pepper and cook for about 5-7 minutes. Arrange 1 chicken patty onto bottom half of each English muffin, followed by some of the apple mixture and 2 cheese slices.

4. Cover with the top halves of English muffins.

5. Cook under the broiler for about 1-2 minutes.

6. Place 1 tbsp of the honey mustard on top of each muffin.

7. Now, place the watercress over each chicken patty and cover with the top halves of English muffins.

8. Enjoy alongside the potato chips.

# *Traditional*
# New England Bread (Molasses and Cornmeal)

🥣 Prep Time: 15 mins
🕐 Total Time: 3 hrs 15 mins

Servings per Recipe: 8
Calories            270.6
Fat                 4.1g
Cholesterol         0.7mg
Sodium              317.7mg
Carbohydrates       50.4g
Protein             7.2g

## Ingredients

1 1/2 lb. loaf
1 1/4 C. water
1/4 C. nonfat dry milk powder
1 tsp salt
3 tbsp light molasses
2 tbsp vegetable oil
3 1/4 C. bread flour

1/3 C. cornmeal
1 1/4 tsp bread machine yeast

## Directions

1. In the bread machine pan, place all the ingredients in the order as suggested by the manual.
2. Select the Basic Cycle and press the Start button.
3. After the completion of cycle, immediately transfer the bread onto a wire rack to cool before slicing.
4. Cut into desired sized slices and enjoy.

# VERMONT
# Pierogies

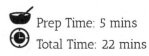

Prep Time: 5 mins
Total Time: 22 mins

Servings per Recipe: 4
Calories              298.4
Fat                   20.7g
Cholesterol           48.8mg
Sodium                571.6mg
Carbohydrates         20.5g
Protein               10.4g

## Ingredients

1 tsp Old Bay Seasoning
1/2 medium head green cabbage, quartered
2 ears corn, each halved
1 1/2 tbsp butter

1 (12 oz.) boxes frozen pierogis, cooked
8 oz. beef kielbasa, sliced thick

## Directions

1. In a Dutch oven, add the seasoning and 1 C. of the water and cook until boiling.
2. Add the 1/2 tbsp of the butter, kielbasa, corn and cabbage and cook, covered for about 9-10 minutes, mixing twice.
3. Add the remaining butter and pierogis and toss to combine.
4. Enjoy hot.

# Cocoa Pudding
# Massachusetts

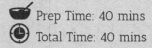 Prep Time: 40 mins

Total Time: 40 mins

Servings per Recipe: 4
| | |
|---|---|
| Calories | 289.8 |
| Fat | 4.8g |
| Cholesterol | 4.2mg |
| Sodium | 408.3mg |
| Carbohydrates | 59.3g |
| Protein | 3.3g |

## Ingredients

Dry Ingredients
1/2 C. flour
1 tsp baking powder
1/2 tsp salt
1/3 C. sugar
1 tbsp cocoa
Wet Ingredients
1/2 C. milk
1 tbsp melted shortening
1/2 tsp vanilla

Topping
1/2 C. brown sugar
2 tbsp cocoa
Topping 2
3/4 C. boiling water

## Directions

1. Set your oven to 350 degrees F before doing anything else and grease a 9x9-inch baking dish.
2. In a bowl, add the flour, sugar, 1 tbsp of the cocoa powder, baking powder and salt and mix well.
3. Now, sift the flour mixture into a second bowl.
4. Add the shortening, milk and vanilla and mix until well combined.
5. For the topping: in another bowl, add the brown sugar and 2 tbsp of the cocoa powder and mix well.
6. Place the mixture into the prepared baking dish evenly and top with the brown sugar mixture.
7. Gently, place the boiling water on top.
8. Cook in the oven for about 30-35 minutes.
9. Enjoy warm.

# AMERICAN
# Cranberry Cobbler

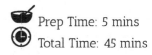 Prep Time: 5 mins

Total Time: 45 mins

Servings per Recipe: 6
| | |
|---|---|
| Calories | 281.4 |
| Fat | 20.6g |
| Cholesterol | 75.9mg |
| Sodium | 111.3mg |
| Carbohydrates | 22.8g |
| Protein | 2.9g |

## Ingredients

1/2 C. unsalted butter, softened
1 1/2 C. cranberries
1/3 C. pecans, toasted, chopped
1/3 C. sugar
1 large egg

1/2 C. all-purpose flour
1/4 tsp salt

## Directions

1. Set your oven to 325 degrees F before doing anything else and grease bottom and halfway up sides of an 8-inch square glass baking dish with 2 tbsp of the butter.
2. In the bottom of the prepared baking dish, place the cranberries evenly and top with the pecans, followed by 1/3 C. of the sugar.
3. In a pan, add the remaining 6 tbsp of the butter over medium-low heat and cook until melted completely.
4. Remove from the heat and keep aside.
5. In the bowl of an electric mixer, fitted with the whisk attachment, add the remaining sugar and egg and beat on medium-high speed until thick and pale. Now, set the speed on medium-low.
6. Slowly, add the flour and salt and beat until well combined.
7. Slowly, add the melted butter and beat until smooth.
8. Place the flour mixture over the cranberries evenly.
9. Cook in the oven for about 45 minutes or until a toothpick inserted in the center comes out clean.
10. Remove from the oven and keep onto the wire rack to cool in the pan for about 10 minutes. Carefully, invert the cake onto the wire rack to cool completely.
11. Enjoy warm.

# Blackstone
# Corn Fritters

Prep Time: 10 mins
Total Time: 20 mins

Servings per Recipe: 6
| | |
|---|---|
| Calories | 131.4 |
| Fat | 2.1g |
| Cholesterol | 38.1mg |
| Sodium | 311.2mg |
| Carbohydrates | 24.1g |
| Protein | 4.7g |

## Ingredients

1 C. flour, sifted
1 1/2 tsp baking powder
1/2 tsp salt
1 egg, well beaten
1/2 C. milk

1 C. corn, cream style
1 tsp grated onion

## Directions

1. In a bowl, add the flour, salt and baking powder.
2. Now, sift the flour mixture into a second bowl.
3. In another bowl, add the milk, egg and corn and beat until well combined.
4. Add the flour mixture and mix until just combined.
5. Fold in the onion.
6. Place a greased skillet over heat until heated through.
7. With a small spoon, place the mixture and cook for about 3-4 minutes, flipping once half way through.